C0-AZS-963

Max-Pol
Fouchet

Rescued Treasures of Egypt

by
Max-Pol Fouchet

McGraw-Hill Book Company · New York · Toronto

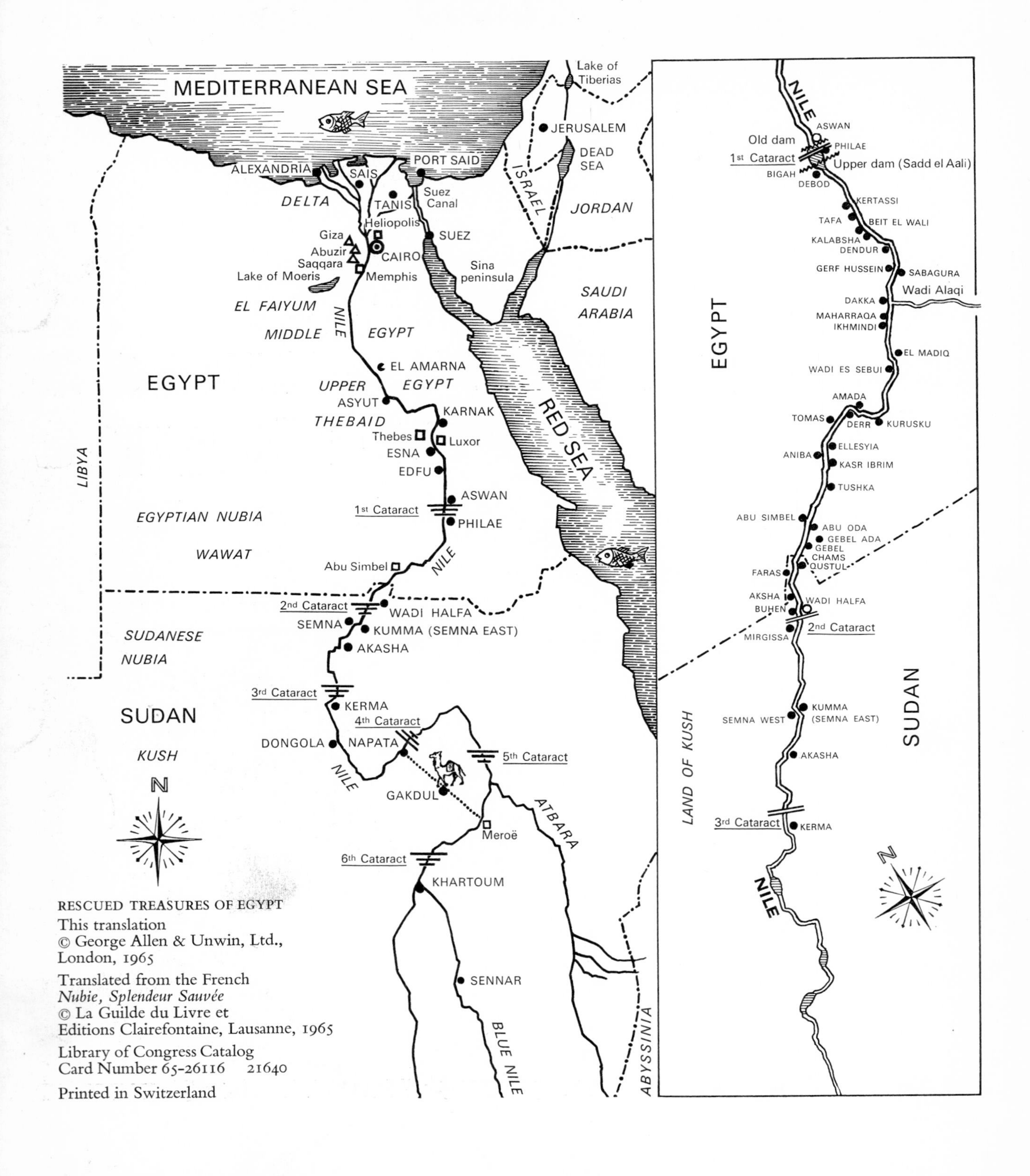

RESCUED TREASURES OF EGYPT
This translation

Translated from the French
Nubie, Splendeur Sauvée

Library of Congress Catalog
Card Number 65-26116 21640

Printed in Switzerland

Contents

Photographs by the author

Translated from the French by Michael Heron

4 ►

5

6

To the Nile

(Egypt. About 2000 B.C.)

Glory to thee, father of life!
Secret god from the secret darkness,
Thou floodest the fields created by the Sun.
Thou quenchest the thirst of the flocks,
Thou waterest the earth.
Celestial path, thou descendest from the heights.
Friend of corn, who makest the seeds to grow.
O God who revealest,
lighten our dwelling-places!

Let men's hands rest:
Thou workest for thy millions of children
If thou subsidest,
it is the downfall of the gods and men
Become frailer than their shadows.
When thou shinest, when thy gifts descend,
The earth trembles with joy,
Everything is reborn,
everything receives nourishment,
Every mouth is filled with food.

Dispenser of exquisite viands,
Thou distributest all good things.
Thou watchest over the sacrifices.
The odour which mounts from thy waters
Is a lordly incense.
When thy waters irrigate two countries,
The corn flows in the granaries.

No dwelling-place can contain thee.
And who could reach thy heart?
Thou hast drunk the tears of all eyes.
Now thou watchest the ripening of the benefits
With which thou hast fortified the generations.
Thou art the lord of the south.
Thy laws are unchangeable in the North.

Thou hast created the evening and the hour of the zenith.
Thou hast drawn their face.
The fulfilment
Of oblations, words carved on stone and pious hopes
Is in thy care.

Thy wrath is terrible and spreads misfortune abroad.
Then, from Thebes to the Delta,
All is a weeping and a distress.
Men go clad in rags,
The divine cycle is broken.

No sooner hast thou answered with
the rising of thy waters
Than the universe is filled with spices.
Thou who establishest order, men praise thee
So that thou repliest and thy waters mount.

O Nile, we have beseeched thee.
Hear the sound of our lutes!
With our hands we sing to thee.
Thou hast heaped joy on thy faithful.
Radiant brightness, thou art our shield.
Thou revivest our hearts.
Thou rejoicest in manifold births.

O overflowing Nile, to thee are dedicated
The sacrifices, the cattle which are slaughtered,
And it is thou whom the hymns extol.
For thee we have immolated birds,
We have lit the sacrificial fire,
O thou whose name the sky steals
And whose appearance no image can capture.

O Nile who dispensest joy to men,
The gods, full of fear, pay homage to the god.
Arise, Nile, let your voice resound,
O Nile, arise, make thy voice heard!

(After Adolf Erman, *La Religion des Egyptiens*, Payot.)

Bread and Stones

When the deadly peril which suddenly faced the monuments of ancient Nubia was revealed, everybody who looks on the works of man as landmarks illuminating the common destiny of all mankind, regardless of the civilisation or religion which produced them, was passionately concerned.
Bas-reliefs, statues and temples were going to disappear beneath the waters. Even on the eve of the event many people still did not realise how serious it was, but the alarm, spread by every possible medium, did not only affect that genuine respect for art which still exists in our contemporary conscience, in spite of attitudinizing and ignorance. Its impact went further. Clearly or confusedly, the threat was felt as a challenge. These glorious remains had to be saved, not only for their beauty, but also for the meaning the rescue operation itself would acquire.
An unhappily divided world, always ready to succumb to its divisions, suddenly had the opportunity to band together to save the treasures of a people and so prove that they belonged to all peoples. Is our age so fertile in sowing destruction, so good at inventing the tools for future disasters, being inconsistent? Is it eager to use these circumstances as attenuating ones? Does it imagine that, by a sort of propitiatory magic, it is protecting itself from ruin by preserving dead ruins? It will have saved some ancient temples, at a time when it has just wiped out others with bombs – and while it was preparing even greater destruction. Future historians will have grounds for astonishment.
Perhaps they will be no less astonished that it needed so many appeals, so much insistence to obtain from the various countries the funds necessary to perpetuate peaceful monuments, when the same countries were wantonly squandering other resources on sowing the sky with poisonous umbels of explosions. If the tall statues of Abu Simbel were to manifest themselves as the effigy of the Commander in *Don Juan*, there would be no guarantee that the villains would repent.

◂ 7

But it is not enough to be entranced by the stones worn by the sun, on the banks of a timeless river with the desert surrounding them, they demand that we make a strict self-examination.

In his speech calling for their rescue, M. André Malraux proclaimed, 'Egypt, then, survives by virtue of certain forms'. It was enough to say that these forms in Nubia ought to be saved. However, if we are not convinced of this by museums and archaeological sites, we perceive it from another survival: that of Egyptian man, less different today from his ancestors than scholars would have us believe. On the banks of the river, in the villages, the simple movement of a peasant working the *shaduf,* the elementary well, the animals of a flock under the raised staff of a shepherd, the profile of a little girl with her eyes prolonged by make-up, we do not discover these things, we rediscover them as something tangible of which we possess only admirable simulacra. Pieces of ancient knowledge, from painted walls or sculptured rocks – suddenly breathing, their rags moving, the dust of their feet on the paths of sand! Legend abounds in human beings turned into statues, in statues becoming human again. This movement to and from (in which a major function of art perhaps resides) is as natural in Egypt as the passage of the feluccas from one bank to another.
Undoubtedly, as M. André Malraux goes on, 'At their highest expression Egyptian conventions were designed to mediate between ephemeral men and the controlling stars'. It is so with all stylistic conventions, especially when they are bound up with religious cultures. But in Egypt, however dominant the presence of the sacred may be, would not one hesitate to state that 'the forms... are not to be interpreted in terms of the living people they profess to portray, but in terms of the conventions which raise these people to the other world'? In our view, that is to neglect excessively the interplay between the country and its arts, between mortals and the symbols of immortality, between the visible world and the other world. Does not such an imperious intellectual decision undermine the more modest and patient approach to works by way of 'ephemeral' human beings? We fear some loss of vibrant flesh, of human clay. Egypt has peopled our childhood and our adult life with images which would only belong to a dream world if living men were not immanent in them. Fortunately they are there, to make art into something other than a dream: a reality. The threat to the monuments of Nubia forces us not to separate living men from their ancient images, an existing people from its legendary style.
One evening, upstream from Asyut.... The raised road dominated the country which was invaded by the flood, a vast windowpane reflecting the sky, broken up by small dykes and spotted with scattered hovels at water level. To rejoin them, the peasants pulled their *gallabieh* up round their waists and plunged thighdeep into the mud, sometimes carrying a child on their shoulders. Flocks of white birds covered the rare hillocks above the floods. In the nearby village, where we were trying to get our car repaired, a man was dead.
Inside the mud hut the man's body was laid out on a stretcher ill concealed by a cotton cloth from which his legs protruded, still coated with flaking mud. His parents and neighbours were seated on the ground outside the door. From inside rose the litany of an old man. The name of Allah recurred in it, taken up in chorus by the women.
It was a bitter day which was drawing to a close. The men of the village had been trying to reinforce the mud walls of an irrigation reservoir, but the flood surprised them by its abundance and by arriving sooner than they had expected. Some immediately set about consolidating the dykes. Others formed a

rampart with their bodies against the wall of the reservoir to enable their companions to perform this task. Propped against the threatened wall, they tried to strengthen it with their arms and legs spread apart, their palms open, living buttresses. The wall had given way behind one of them. The man had fallen into the reservoir under a heap of mud. He had been freed, but too late. Now he lay in the hut, fashioned of earth, one would have said, like those statuettes of Osiris in which the Egyptians used to sow seeds, waiting for them to grow green, as a sign of rebirth.
A fellah dead, as many others have died during the life-giving flood, since the Nile has been the Nile.

2

Since the Nile has been the Nile... Over and over again we were told at school that Egypt is 'a gift of the Nile'. How could we imagine the long hardship, the sacrifices required of the recipients of the gift, all those men in uncertainty, from the ancient Egyptians, who dug the first channels to lead the flood water further away, down to this dead fellah? True, we knew about the works of the Pharaohs, but the words of Herodotus left the deepest impression: 'Nowadays – which is not the case with the rest of humanity – the Egyptians do not have to do any work to cultivate their land; they have no furrow to plough, no hoe to wield, none of the exhausting tasks which men perform to earn their daily bread: the river comes of its own accord to water their fields, withdraws in the same way and each man has only to sow the ground and let his pigs loose on it. The latter, by trampling the soil, finally press the seeds into it and there is nothing more to do but await the harvest. It is trodden by the pigs, the pigs are taken home, the job is done!'
Perhaps it was the memory of this Eden-like vision which first came back to people when they learnt that the waters of a new dam would accumulate and immerse the relics of ancient Egypt in Nubia? Was it necessary to build this iconoclastic monster? Wasn't it out of proportion? Wasn't it a purely political project? Couldn't it be done in a *different* way? We can witness to these reactions. We learnt them by letter or by word of mouth when we were trying to alert good will by a film. But perhaps it would have been answer enough if our interlocutors could have seen the body of a dead fellah inside four mud walls upstream from Asyut, one anonymous evening.

The necessity of the new dam – the Sadd el Aali – emerged from the facts. They have been stated; yet they have to be repeated in the preface to a book in which the gods and their stone images will take up the story afterwards. These facts show in our contemporary men – and it is not the look of the ancient gods which weighs heaviest on us, but the look of living men honed sharp, like knives, by hunger and fever.
Facts? Here is the first one: the 'useful' surface of Egypt is equivalent to about the area of Belgium, but 9 million inhabitants live on the latter against 26 million on the former (1960 census). To this must be added the galloping demography of the Egyptian population. It rose from 10 million in 1897 to 13 million in 1917 and 19 million in 1947 – to reach the figure we have quoted, revealing an astonishing acceleration. Between 1947 and 1960 the rate of increase was estimated at 2.5%. To feed those who live, to feed those who are born, to feed those who will be born. That is the problem for Egypt today: to feed the people or let them die.

The first advance would be to ensure the maximum yield from land already productive. The Nile has a potentate's caprices:

frequently it provides too much or not enough. Its annual mean yield of 84 milliard cubic metres may reach a total of 150 milliard cubic metres – and fall as low as 48 milliards in certain lean years. If there is a plethora, the river inundates, submerges, destroys. If there is a shortage, drought prevails. The fellah of Asyut was the victim of an excess of water; he could equally well have succumbed to the consequences of a drought.
It is necessary to regulate the whims of the river. The solution is to stock its waters in such a way that the reserve, from one year to another, is constant and large enough to meet deficiencies. When the flood is poor, the necessary addition will be borrowed from the volume accumulated. If there is an excess, the surplus will be disposed of. The old Aswan dam can no longer claim to perform this role of regulation and distribution satisfactorily. For a long time Egypt's urgent needs have exceeded its capacity. It will have to make way for the new plant which is to meet them.

Moreover the Nile is prodigal. It squanders its wealth: 45% of its waters are lost in the sea. Here we pass from the first objective to the second, from the intensive and regular working of land already cultivated to the cultivation of new land, indispensable for the subsistence of a constantly increasing population. Egypt possesses this land, but it needs water. The old dam formed a reservoir with a capacity of 5 milliard cubic metres. *The Sadd el Aali will have a capacity of 150 milliard cubic metres.* Is there any need to dwell on the difference? Mr. Ivan Komzine, one of the Soviet engineers called in to construct the dam, describes the consequences. The water of the Nile will not be uselessly lost in the Mediterranean. The colossal mass of water – nine times that of Lake Léman, according to our technician – will enable Egypt to win more than 1,976,840 acres by the continuous irrigation of new ground; in other words to increase its cultivable surface by 30% [1].
It is anticipated that the same area will be doubled in the Nubian part of the Republic of the Sudan.
To feed the people is the fundamental task, but the living must be enabled to make a living, they must be guaranteed work. In this field Egypt, already fundamentally a farming country, cannot expect everything from agriculture. Now its efforts are aimed at mechanising its activities, from the craftsman's workshop to the factory and heavy industry. Without coal, forced to import its fuel, it has to call on electrification for its energy. Again the Sadd el Aali provides the solution. By supplying a very powerful hydroelectric works with its waters, it will generate about 9 milliard kwh annually at a low price. 'The power available to the U.A.R. is thus multiplied by more than four' (Komzine). Then we understand the naive inscriptions often found on walls: 'The Sadd el Aali is our father.'
We have confined ourselves to the basic human needs. There are others. To many they will seem to be purely political. In our view they cannot be separated from the first. Egypt is now independent. To ensure that her independence is not artificial, to escape from the status of the pretty kept woman, she is forced to exploit her personal resources. She has iron ore useful for her industry: at Aswan, in particular. The regulation of the Nile will make it possible to send it more easily, by the river route, to the industrial centres of the North, to the big blast furnaces at Helwan, near Cairo, for example. If we add this advantage to the returns obtained

[1] From a book on the dam by Ivan Komzine, Professor at the Institute of Civil Engineering at Kuibyshev (Moscow, 1964). On the whole we have used the figures supplied in this work, which is frankly propagandist. Incidentally, these figures differ little from those found in other books, even when written from the opposite or an independent point of view. Sometimes they are actually lower.

8 ▸

from the extension of agriculture, to the profits accruing from the manufacture on the national territory of the fertilizers necessary for it, to the savings in foreign exchange resulting from the decrease in purchases from abroad – purchases of coal and fuel oil, in particular, since the old steam generating stations will be increasingly replaced by hydro-electric generating stations – how can we fail to foresee a favourable transformation in the Egyptian economy? As an appendix to this book, the reader will find figures, statistics and supplementary technical information. They would only burden this introduction in which we are confining ourselves to the essential facts. However, we may note this striking estimate: the national income, thanks to the Sadd el Aali, will increase by 355 milliards annually, the Treasury by 23 milliards.[1] The global cost of the so-called 'Fifteen Year Plan' (construction of the dam and the generating station; improvement of land, the irrigation network and drainage; electrification of the countryside) is evaluated at 1,300 milliards. Allowing for an excess of optimism, the operation is, to use a popular expression, a *paying* one.

'A thousand sluices would master and distribute the flood water. In every part of the national territory the eight or ten million cubic fathoms of water which are lost annually in the sea would be distributed in all the low-lying parts of the desert, as far as the oases and much farther west. A large number of fire-engines and windmills would raise the waters into water towers, from which they would be drawn for irrigation. Under a good administration the Nile is victorious over the desert, under a bad one, the desert is victorious over the Nile...'

Thus spoke Napoléon Bonaparte in 1800, when the country numbered barely 3 million inhabitants.

Even if the 'thousand sluices' make us smile today, at least the firm intention to give Egypt the indispensable water is contained in these words. In any case the project is not new. On the other hand, the approval accompanying it, the enthusiasm supporting it, are new; the enthusiasm and approval of a whole people. There is a *mystique* of the dam, which is at once naive and thought out, spontaneous and controlled. We have observed it not only where it was natural to find it, in political circles, in certain intellectual circles, on the sites, but also in the street of a town or a village during a chance encounter, when the three magic words Sadd el Aali suddenly kindled a spark in someone's eyes. Between Aswan and Abu Simbel, with our boat at anchor for the night, alongside the bank condemned to disappear, how many times have I not heard the Nubian chants of the crew break off and give way to the 'Song of the High Dam':

We built the Pyramids,
We shall build the Sadd el Aali.

The simple effect of propaganda, one might say. Perhaps, but is that explanation enough? For a people so recently subject to a colonial 'presence', are there not grounds for considering this immense task with pride, as a proof of vitality? The fact that it required the decisive collaboration of a foreign power, without which it could not have been undertaken, does not lessen this pride, since it was by playing on the rivalry between the powers of East and West that Egypt obtained the help of one of them and at the same time

[1] Figures taken from different books and reports, in particular from the intelligent book by Simone Lacouture: *Egypte* (Ed. du Seuil, 1962). More recently, the newspaper *Le Monde* (24 July 1964) published a study (undoubtedly of semi-official origin) which said: 'The Sadd el Aali will increase the country's annual income by 234 million Egyptian pounds.' Mr. Komzine *(op. cit.)* gives other estimates: the national income will increase by 235–250 million Egyptian pounds, i.e. an increase of 35%.

asserted her political realism. After all, peoples first prove themselves as peoples by their great collective works: the road or the bridge, the cathedral or the dam.

It is not a wall which is going to dam the Nile, about 4 miles upstream from Aswan, but a giant prism. The sandy bottom prevented the stone bedding of heavy masonry for the foundations. So the solution of the 'dam-weight' was chosen: 43 million cubic metres of material were brought and piled up to form the obstructing mass. On the bed first consolidated, a conglomerate of sand, gravel, granite and clay surrounds a watertight curtain which penetrates to the crystalline shield. Six thousand workers will have worked on this task, often instructed on the actual site by Soviet and Egyptian technicians. The thickness of the dam at the base will be about 3,215 feet and at the top 131 feet. Its height will be some 364 feet. According to Komzine, its length at the top will be about 3 miles.

'We built the Pyramids, we shall build the Sadd el Aali...' An exaggerated comparison? The High Dam will have a volume seventeen times that the largest pyramid, the Pyramid of Cheops.

Moreover the Sadd el Aali has its own history which merges with part of the history of our time. Let us recall the events closest to us. In 1954, Gamal Abdel Nasser, president of the Republic after the 'resignation' of General Neguib, decided on the construction of the dam: in December under the direction of Egyptian engineers (Mr. Moussa Arafa, Dr. Hassan Abbas Zaki, among others), with the help of foreign firms (Sugrea: French; Alexander Gibbs and Partners: English; the Hochtief und Dortmund Union; German) the preparatory studies, already begun some years earlier, were nearly finished. In 1955 the first work was initiated. On 19 July 1956, the United States went back on their promise of a credit of 56 million dollars to finance it; the next day Great Britain also cancelled her offer of 15 million dollars; the International Bank followed suit and withdrew the 200 million dollars allocated a week previously. On 26 July President Nasser retorted: the International Suez Canal Company was nationalised, its profits would be used to build the dam. Alas, we know the result. On 29 October the war between Israel and Egypt broke out; on 30 October came the 'intervention' of England and France which ended to their disadvantage in a cease-fire in November.

In December 1958, by the terms of the first agreement, the USSR undertook to supply the aid necessary for the construction of a preliminary stage of the work. As soon as this agreement was ratified in January 1959, specialists from the Hydroproject Institute in Moscow were on the job; new solutions were proposed and adopted. In January 1960 the first charge of explosives pulverised the first mass of rock, the real signal that work had begun. The 1958 agreement was considerably enlarged. In May 1964 President Nasser and Nikita Kruschchev pressed the button which made the Nile flow into the diversion channel. According to the estimates, the Sadd el Aali should be finished in 1968.

An immense sheet of water will cover a distance of some 312 miles – i.e. 218 miles in Egyptian Nubia and 94 in Sudanese Nubia – upstream from Aswan to Aksha. At some points it will be as much as 12 to 16 miles wide. The Egyptian part will be called Lake Nasser.

Then the Nubian Nile will rise from 397 feet above sea level, the elevation reached by the old dam at the period of the high waters, to the *constant* level of 597 feet, i.e. 200 feet higher.

Then Nubia will have disappeared. As a sort of sacrifice.

3

It is possible that Lower Nubia, as a whole, could easily disillusion the lover of 'unforgettable sites'. Apart from the region of the cataracts and the few places where the strangled river has fought to win a passage, the décor was rarely masterly, the stage setting rarely romantic. You sailed along the Nile between two deserts, but almost as soon as you were aware of them the feeling of space turned into a sort of familiarity, of accessible proximity. Some lively minds have experienced boredom between Aswan and Wadi Halfa, finding the stretch tedious. It was not our experience. On each journey Nubia captivated us.

How? The landscape was so often absence of landscape. The same sandstone banks continued on either side of the river, without any really picturesque indentations. At low water the yellowish watermark left by the floods was exposed; its endless straight line had a hypnotic effect. When the sandstone gave way to granite, the incident became important, as any occurrence acquires importance in a day free of incident. In another place the rock was interrupted and a sand-dune sloped down, flowed down, molten metal at midday, soft silk at the advent of twilight. The sand was still piled up at the mouth of an old wadi, long without water; it was one of those *khors* which opened out in dried out faults, in arid theatres. With a little luck, as night approached, you might see pieces of mud detach themselves from the mud, move, slide towards the water and dive into it: small crocodiles frightened by the noise of the propeller.

At long intervals, the two mountain ranges, the Arabian and the Libyan, sent down their spurs. Their shapes seemed strange, so little strangeness was there in the surroundings. They reached the river as isolated mounds or groups of hillocks, which seemed made to announce the first pink of dawn and the last pink of the day on their summits, to turn some patches of ground mauve or blue and to prove that natural volumes did exist beside these banks whose surface was so flat. To love the 'landscape' of Nubia you must love the slow way it unfolds and with its sham monotony produces the feeling of a duration outside time, even love the lack of episodes in which the mind can abandon itself to a thought without thought, more fecundating than it seems, perhaps susceptible of leading to the Other Side. You must love recitative.

These austere banks were not uninhabited. Let us admit our surprise on an early journey: on the slope of the banks, on the ridges, in the rare plains, on the edge of the plateau, the villages were spaced out, never very far apart. Only the regions which were too rocky had none. Their houses are conceived very simply: low, elongated, geometrical, dominated by the brief phallic minaret of the mosque. They had very few openings on the outside, but the narrow doors, the rare windows – it would be more accurate to write 'openings' since they generally had no shutters – faced the Nile, dark holes from which our passage was watched. If it was a large residence the door became the ornamental portal of a vast interior courtyard: children suddenly appeared in it, like a bunch of grapes.

10, 11

During the journey there were fewer villages to accompany us than houses. There were isolated examples perched on a peak or snuggled in a hollow in the rock, like solitary relay stations. From afar they seemed no more than waist high. Sometimes they merged with the soil, built as they were of mud or of blocks of sand stone pointed with mud; more often they stood out from it, for Nubia liked to rough-cast its walls in white.

Shall I ever forget this country? It is surprising to find so many villages but so few signs of life. Ruined villages? 12, 14
Abandoned houses? Abandoned sites? No, just very few people in them. However, there is a little girl on the bank: she stops filling a pitcher, waves a vague greeting, resumes her task, then climbs the steep bank and her red dress is lost among the stones. Farther off, much farther off, is a group of women, all dressed in black: the Nubian shadow is never as dark as the womens' veils. Once again the bank continues for a long time without a soul. Then a donkey emerges, making a detour round some fallen debris. It carries two burdens: its master and the sun. Elsewhere, we see some goats, but without their goatherd, their colours in harmony with the mixture of ochres, beiges, pale yellows, browns, greys and pinkish tones of the environment. Rare apparitions. Rare as the trees: with the exception of two or three oases – (oasis of Ballana! praised be thy sheikh with the lean face of the conqueror! you were a garden of Eden!) – you have to be satisfied with thorny bushes and obstinate palmtrees which are immersed almost to the top of their trunks at the time of the high waters, only their palms forming a bouquet above the surface of the stream.
So many villages, but such a restricted life. To find the reason you must land on the bank. When the waters are high the houses touch the river. At the period of low water, they are perched again; to reach them you first cross the cracked mud, then the beds of pebbles and lastly you climb the escarpment. Young boys and girls come down to meet you. Since Nubia in peril has attracted more and more tourists and scholars, the children, have learnt to greet them in French, German Italian and even Spanish, and when your reply has told them your nationality, listen to them laugh! They do not offer to sell you anything, for the simple reason that they have nothing to sell, except the skin of a viper of the sand dunes or some large lizard, still alive, but dazed by hunger and the torments of the children. Nor do they beg. This is not a Nubian habit. If you meet a woman in the village she passes quickly, slips into a house and hides her black silhouette in the black of the interior. The old men are more loquacious, inclined to a solemn but circumspect welcome. Arabic is very little spoken in Nubia, in spite of the efforts of the government, except in the region of Wadi es Sebui, where Libyan tribes have settled. Qensi predominates downstream from this 'islet' as far as Aswan; upstream, Uba. The Nubians have their own language which the people of Egypt do not understand, as they have their own way of life, their traditions, their songs which differ both from Arab music and the rhythmic chant of negro Africa.

Children, women, old men... But what about the young people, the young and middle-aged men? You will be surprised how few there are. It is no use looking for them. If you do happen to meet one you learn that he is on a visit to his people and will soon be off again. The men of Nubia are elsewhere. They have had to become expatriates to earn a living for their families, to go to the north and the towns, to Cairo, Alexandria, Port Said and Suez. There they work as domestic servants, porters, watchmen, and are much sought after, for the honesty of the Nubians is widely known and celebrated by right of tradition. They also work as waiters in the big hotels where they serve stimulating coffee or iced drinks to the tourists exhausted by pyramids, hypogeums and museums. Their fine stature and their carnation blackness, when they are dolled up in the rig-out of an oriental operetta, impress the English spinsters, French bourgeoisie and German *doktors*. They are called 'Barbarins', a distortion of 'Barabbrah', the name of a section of their race, and of 'Berberi'. The Barbarins send their families food parcels and money. As soon as they can they go to spend a few days with their families, get to know the children born since their last visit, help in the work of the village and then leave again for the north. That is why Nubia, as an author has accurately defined it, is 'the country of women without men'.

What else could it be? Before the construction of the first Aswan dam, when the Nile flowed in its ancient bed, the valley had a fringe on either side on which lupin, sorghum and broad beans (so necessary for *ful,* the national dish) were cultivated. This fringe – sometimes narrow, sometimes wide, when it extended across into a plain or took advantage of the recession of the rocky banks – disappeared with the formation of the first artificial storage lake. However the Nubians did not despair. They rebuilt their houses and villages on the banks, away from the high waters. The first dam did not compel an exodus.

Nor did the way it functioned deprive them of subsistence altogether. For nine months, from October to June, it held back the waters, creating the artificial lake whose level rose, we may recall, to 397 feet above sea level. Then came the season of the floods. After the flood of the 'Green' Nile, when the flood of the 'Red' Nile, rich in the ferruginous alluvial materials of Abyssinia, was announced, the sluices opened so that Egypt received the indispensable flood. Then the reservoir emptied, the level dropped. So, as far as Nubia was concerned, the flood retreated. A ribbon of earth reappeared between the limit of the high waters and that of the low waters. A wretched reappearance, true, and of short duration: three months every year! But during these months it was possible to farm, if one hurried. Between the beginning of July and the end of September everything had to take place: sowing, ripening, harvesting. This poor harvest, which had to be disputed with the birds, was insufficient and the men emigrated so that their native land would survive.

The Nubians' attachment to their soil was shown when the rumour spread of a new submersion, due to a new dam. This time the Nile would never reveal the temporary fields, since the level would stay permanently high. Nubia would disappear. At first the news was received with scepticism, then came anger and confusion. Of course the Nubians were assured that they would be transported elsewhere, settled on more fertile land. They would live by themselves in villages built for them around Kom Ombo and Esna. These promises did not appease the sorrow or reduce the obstinacy of this little race. The old men often said they would rather die where they were than abandon their birthplaces. The days of dilatoriness, in this country where nothing accelerates or devours the time, seemed to justify the incredulous. The rise of the Nile was delayed. Many rough-cast their houses again as if nothing threatened them.

An author has written pertinently of the Nubian civilisation, 'all display is concentrated on the habitat. The Nubians know how to give the absolute bareness of their houses the poetry of a vanished dream, with a very sure aesthetic sense and a fertile imagination' (S. Lacoutre, *op. cit.*). It is their bareness which gives the houses their simple volumes, harmonising so well with the violent light and the tyranny of the sun. They are sited in a vast play of parallels – that of the river, the rocks and the horizon. This does not mean that no attention is paid to adorning their nudity! Festoons, battlements and mouldings of broken lines often decorate the tops of the façades. Sometimes, on the white rough-casting of the walls, there are bouquets, birds, animals, boats, aeroplanes (escapees, one would say, from the Douanier Rousseau's studio!) or more ambitious 'compositions', illustrating a theme of official propaganda, the journey to Mecca of a man of the village, a legendary tale: paintings with vivid colours, drawings by a naive intelligence, images which remind us of those decorating certain Indian houses at Benares where, as here, the walls are like the white pages of an exercise book, all illustrated by the marriage of likeness and allegory.

64

Mirrors? On many façades regularly arranged circles flash – and you discover on closer inspection that they are plates, round saucers which reflect the light. These pieces of china are embedded in the outside wall to embellish it. They bear coats of arms, the names of palaces: here is china from the Semiramis, from Shepheard's at Cairo, from the Mena House at Giza and the Windsor at Alexandria. The men of Nubia bring them back on return visits to their country. These items of broken 'services' which they have bought cheaply indicate the hotels where they have worked or still work. Medals, if you like, to show that they do not serve just anybody, signs of dignity, but even more medallions, the ornamentation of these dwellings where only bowls are used. During my last stay I returned to a village where certain houses were decorated like this, with the most curious effect. They were, alas, deserted; their inhabitants had been evacuated in anticipation of the arrival of the high water. The rough-casting of the walls was still a vivid white, but the plates had been loosened and taken away. A dull empty circle marked the spot where they had once been. The façades no longer flashed, they had lost their touch of fantasy. They seemed to have empty eye-sockets.

14

I remember a conversation with Professor Torgny Säve-Söderbergh of the University of Upsala in 1960, when we were passing some still inhabited villages. A specialist in Nubian ethnography, he could not prevent a note of bitterness from creeping into his remarks. 'Archaeologists', he said, 'are too preoccupied with rescuing essential archaeological monuments to be seriously concerned about the disappearance of a race and a civilisation. But we must not forget that Nubian is still spoken as far as the Fourth Cataract. Will the Nubian peoples be able to live elsewhere without losing their originality? Their personality will finally be wiped out in the Egyptian masses. It is commonly believed that the Nubians are negroes because they have black skins. Yet they have no negroid characteristics. From the anthropological point of view, it is impossible to distinguish between the skeletons of ancient Egyptians and those of the Nubians. Save the temples, yes. But what is going to disappear is a civilisation which is situated between negro Africa in the south and white Africa in the north. It owed its own importance, its specificity, to this situation. Are we not forgetting something essential? What counts is the knowledge of *human* history.'

I hear those words again each time I see the slow rising and falling of the river, as I imagine too I can hear the noise of the engines of the small boats which carried me, the *Taouaf,* the *Sheikh el Beled,* the companions of my amazement and meditation. Nubian pilots sailed these boats. The eddies and sands of the Nile were as familiar to them as the villages which they greeted with a toot on the siren to advise some relation that they were passing.

Should we be upset, it will be asked, by the obliteration of a poor country, without great charm and long unable to provide its men with a living? Besides, the Nubians were not numerous: 40,000 to 60,000, according to the estimates. This small people will be settled on good land. Our times have known more tragic transfers of population.

Undoubtedly. In any case, we can no longer write in the present tense. It is already a question of the past. Already only the memory remains. Nubia *was.*

4

Are we being arbitrary in calling the rescued treasures' to which our book is devoted the treasures 'of Egypt', when they are actually situated in Nubia?

The reader can be assured that it is not our intention in this chapter to belittle a clearly defined ethnic and historical personality. You will note that its own characteristics will be emphasised. However, we felt that the style of the Nubian temples was imported to such an extent we could not deal with it on a local basis. The sanctuaries the Pharaohs of Egypt built in Nubia were completely Egyptian and when the national dynasties had to yield their power to foreigners, it was the imitation of ancient models which dominated the building of new temples on the foundations of yesterday. In the same way, during the Christian period, the Nubian churches reflected Byzantine standards and iconograpahy on these remote banks of the Nile. Nubia was predestined for invasion and occupation by its situation, its role as a 'corridor' between Egypt and Africa. These conquerors could do no less than show their presence and their strength by monuments consistent with their genius. The Pharaohs had to 'Egyptianise' Nubia. For its part, Nubia adopted the civilisation of its masters so completely that it prolonged it for a long time, even perpetuating this civilisation which history had condemned to decadence.

Egypt penetrated into Nubia five thousand years ago. A stela found in the Sudan near the Second Cataract, in the indentation of the rocks of Gebel Sheikh Souleiman, reveals the passage of an expedition sent southwards by King Djer. This Pharaoh, until then considered as legendary by many scholars, belonged to the 1st dynasty. Not far away, near Buhen, excavations undertaken by Professor J. Vercoutter revealed an Egyptian necropolis in which seals of the same dynasty were discovered. The kings of the first two dynasties (the Thinite period, –3200 –2780) seem to have been interested in Nubia on both sides of the Second Cataract for reasons of expansion and security, but also for other motives. The art of working gold and ivory became important in this period, which was, in M. Jean Yoyotte's expression, 'the adolescence of the pharaonic world'. It is possible that Nubia was already considered as a producer of the precious metal and a transit zone for African ivory. In any case, its little known peoples (archaeologists designate them under the names of 'groupes A, B and C') still belonged to prehistory when the Egyptians entered history.

During the archaic period, the frontier of Egypt was fixed at the First Cataract – which was an encroachment, since Nubia, to the ancient Egyptians, did not begin at the height of present-day Aswan, but about sixty miles further north, at Edfu. History was going to see the displacement of this frontier southwards, at first as far as the Second Cataract, then further still.

Lower Nubia was occupied during the Old Kingdom, but the countries which extended on either side of the Second Cataract were relatively protected then by their terrifying reputation: they were said to be peopled with phantoms and ghosts. The Pharaohs of the 4th (–2723 –2563) and the 5th dynasty (–2563 –2423), unimpressed by these fables, maintained commercial relations with them. They even sent military expeditions there. Here again archaeology throws light on these undertakings. In 1961–1962, at Buhen, Professor W. B. Emery discovered an industrial centre where copper ore was treated more than four thousand years ago. The crucibles, the moulds and what served as blast furnaces were all found, still spattered with metal. The centre must have been very important about 2600 B.C. The kings of the Old Kingdom obtained their supplies from it, so they had to guarantee the safety of the convoys along the river and the caravan tracks.

In the Middle Kingdom there was a new advance: the frontier was fixed at the Second Cataract. The Egyptians developed 'an aggressive colonial policy' in Nubia. This assertion by the American Egyptologist John A. Wilson[1], is corroborated by many documents, in particular by two stelae of Sesostris III (–1887 –1850), erected at Semna. The Pharaoh does not hide his intentions with regard to the 'Nehsiu', the black peoples of the south. On the first stela, it is stated that the frontier in the south has been established 'to block the passage of any Nehsi travelling northwards, by land or water, and any Nehsiu flocks – unless the Nehsi is travelling for commercial motives or is on an (official) mission or has any other valid motive, always excepting that no boat of the Nehsiu be allowed to pass via Semna going northwards'. The second stela bears witness to the Egyptian's disdain: 'I have fixed my frontier by penetrating further than my fathers; I have increased what was allotted to me... The Nehsiu are not people worthy of respect, they are poor and have no energy. My Majesty has seen them: there is no exaggeration about this.' Such a judgment explains why we can read in a military report that when six natives presented themselves before a fortress to receive some provisions during a period of famine, they were sent off to die of hunger in the desert. A certain Hepzefa, who represented the central authority as 'Governor of the South', was buried at Kerma in circumstances which are worth reporting: 'A funeral feast was given on the occasion at which more than a thousand oxen were slaughtered and their skulls buried to the south outside the enclosing wall. The body of the prince was then placed for his last repose in the vaulted chamber in the midst of offerings and the wooden door was sealed. The victims of the sacrifice – two or three hundred in number, including children

[1] Egypt, Life and Death of a Civilisation.

10 ►

– *all Nubians,* drugged during their last meal, were laid on the ground in the corridor. By their sides, some receptacles, sometimes a sword and their personal ornaments were laid. Then the corridor was filled in, forming a small hillock, which was then covered with sun-baked bricks . . .'[1]

All Nubians. We have underlined these words. Taking local traditions into account, they are enough indication of how the Nubians were treated by their Egyptian masters. The establishment of a trading station at Kerma, south of the Third Cataract, shows that the Egyptians' commercial enterprises in the Middle Empire went beyond the frontier of the Second Cataract. Kerma was situated on the edge of a rich agricultural district; a colony was established there. But the trading station was a veritable fortress, whose defence was entrusted to personages of importance by Hepzefa. The kings of the Middle Kingdom were not deluded, they knew what dangers threatened Upper Nubia, dangers which could rapidly swamp the defences and extend downstream. They busied themselves in strengthening these defences. Thus they added Sudanese mercenaries to their own troops, organising a special corps with them, a kind of constabulary, the Medjai. Better still, they consolidated the old entrenched camps, enlarged the forts and above all built new fortresses. A veritable line of strong places was established along the Second Cataract and further south: Buhen, Mirgissa, Semna West and Semna East (Kumma) – we shall devote a chapter to them and deal at length with Buhen which was rebuilt during the New Kingdom. During this period, unrest grew when other peoples arrived from the south (the archaeologists' group C). The men of these peoples, kept in check at first, soon united their customs with those of the Egyptians and then became so Egyptianised that it was impossible to distinguish them five centuries after their arrival. Thus a grave peril was absorbed, by osmosis and metamorphosis.

[1] Professor G. A. Reisner, *Bulletin of the Museum of Fine Arts,* XIII (Boston, 1915).

◄ 11

What was going to happen under the New Kingdom (–1580 –1090)? Weakened by the feeble governments of the kings who preceded it and divided into two kingdoms once more, Egypt was ravaged by the Asiatic Hyksos. They occupied the delta and a part of the inland territory; they forced the Thebaid to recognise its vassalage. In these difficult conditions Egypt could not prevent Nubia from becoming autonomous again.

The Thebans, relatively independent of the invaders, nevertheless prepared to free the country. They realised that they would have to fight on two fronts: conquer the Asiatics in the north and reconquer the south. Thus King Kamose complains before his courtiers 'of having to share the power with a Negro who dominates Nubia, and an Asiatic who reigns at Avaris'.[1] The Nubians, as was to be expected, were the allies of the Hyksos.

Once the latter were conquered and thrown out of Egypt, the sovereigns of the New Kingdom did not rest until they had punished the Nubians and re-established their domination over the rebel country. A preliminary expedition led by Amosis did not produce lasting results. Revolt broke out soon afterwards and the task had to be resumed by his successors who claimed definitive successes each time. Was it a question of a coherent resistance? Or simply of local rebellions, quickly put down by a police operation? Did the Pharaohs exaggerate the incidents to enhance their exploits and furnish themes for their praise? The depiction of the prostrate Sudanese was part of the official imagery, it was repeated on the temples. 'The long lists of conquered Nubian peoples which decorate the pylons and the representations of the king massacring a negro

[1] E. Drioton and J. Vandier, *L'Egypte* (P.U.F., 1962).

prisoner belong more to the domain of formulas and traditional iconography than to the domain of History'.[1] It is none the less true that the situation in Nubia was by no means settled. That is doubtless why the kings of the 18th and 19th dynasties built, in addition to military installations, many religious foundations where they appeared as the formidable associates of the deities. At Abu Simbel we shall see Ramesses II manifest himself as god *in his lifetime*.

This kind of theological reference would have had no meaning if Nubia had not been Egyptianised. Not only was it profoundly Egyptianised but the kings of the New Kingdom also practised a policy of integrating its élite. After a victory they demanded that the young princes be taken to Thebes. They were habituated to Egyptian civilisation, made to need it, and it was hoped that they would be faithful allies on their return, after this 'brainwashing' and 'conditioning'. Egyptians were quite willing to marry the ladies of the Nubian aristocracy. Later, Nubians of quality were summoned to high posts in the central government and others received honorary appointments.

In the 18th dynasty, the first of the three dynasties which compose the New Kingdom, the office of viceroy of Nubia was created. In principle it was supposed to fall to the king's son so that he could serve his apprenticeship in a far country, but generally it was held by high officials in the royal entourage. The viceroy's authority extended over the two provinces of which Nubia was now made up: *Wawat,* from the First to the Second Cataract, in other words Lower Nubia; the *Land of Kush,* from the Second to the Fourth Cataract, our Sudanese Upper Nubia and its extension. The name of this province figures in the viceroy's appellation: he bears the title of 'Royal Son of Kush'.

Each of the two provinces was administered by a governor, placed under the authority of the viceroy. The latter's powers were considerable. Chief of the flocks, the granary, the Treasury, he was also chief of the police forces and military detachments which had to see to the protection of gold-bearing convoys. He was also head of the religion. He had a large administration under his orders. His office included 'three responsibilities: delegation of the government of the African Empire, exploitation of the Nubian gold mines and command of the African army.' (Wilson, *op. cit.*). We can imagine that such an office must have been coveted, all the more because its remoteness allowed a large measure of autonomy. The 'Royal Son' was the third personage in Egypt, after the Vizier of Upper Egypt and the High Priest of Amun at Karnak. His other titles indicate his dignity: Fan-bearer on the right of the King', 'Chief of the Countries of the South', 'Chief of the Land of Gold of Amun'. In an indirect way, Nubia saw the importance attached to it.

For a long time this policy enabled the Kingdom to extend its authority as far as the Fourth Cataract, but it contained the causes of its own future collapse. In the process of becoming Egyptianised, the Nubian princes did not repudiate Nubia, they learnt methods of liberation and revenge. The adoption by a colonised country of a considerable part of the civilisation of the colonising power does not attach it to the latter, on the contrary it shows it that it can equal it – and from then on separate from it. The absurdity of all colonial domination is that it cannot last without itself creating the circumstances of its abolition. The Egyptian annexation of Nubia was doomed to the fate which awaits all colonial systems. Our contemporary experience may help us to understand this.

But who would have believed that the 'miserable land of Kush', as the contemptuous Pharaohs called it, would provide

[1] E. Drioton and J. Vandier, *L'Egypte* (P.U.F., 1962).

Egypt with a dynasty? And that a 'Negro', to use an inaccurate word, would reign over the whole of Egypt?

Many Nubians were close enough to the last kings of the New Kingdom to see how the royal power was weakening and passing to the High Priests of Amun at Thebes. When one of the latter, a general into the bargain, wiped out Ramesses XI, Nubia hastened the march of time. Henceforth imperious conquering Egypt belonged to the past. Herihor, the usurper, knew the countries of Wawat and Kush; he held the office of viceroy there at the moment when he was going to seize power (–1085). Nubians supported him against the last Ramesside. When the dynasty of Priest-Kings, descendants of Herihor collapsed in its turn (–950) and gave way to the Libyan dynasty, its last representative and the Theban clergy took refuge in Upper Nubia. They reached the region of the Fourth Cataract and settled at Napata, at the foot of the Gebel Barkal. Thus Napata became the capital of an independent and theocratic kingdom, in which the worship of Amun was glorified, as at Thebes.

In fact it was from Napata that king Piankhi set out to conquer Egypt in –730. Were the Nubians waiting for the opportunity? It certainly could not have been more favourable. Kings, rival dynasties and high priests shared the dislocated territory. The weakness which resulted from this division was a pledge of security for the Nubians, but an ambitious prince of the western delta, Tefnakhte of Sais, decided to re-establish Egyptian unity on his own account. When Tefnakhte attacked Middle Egypt, Piankhi went to meet him. In the war which followed, the Nubian gave proof of strategic abilities which secured him the victory. The whole of Egypt submitted to a king of Nubia. History has its curious ups and downs.

A strange personage, Piankhi! Sometimes his expedition resembled a crusade, or at least a pilgrimage under arms. During the journey, he never forgot to honour the local gods and allot half the booty to the temples. The religion of ancient Egypt had been maintained intact, preserved in the distant withdrawn kingdom of Napata. So the Nubian king appeared as a man concerned about the faith, restoring – he, the foreigner! – the ancient strictness. 'His chivalrous conduct of the war, his austerity which kept him away from the beautiful captives, his love of horses, the scrupulousness with which he carried out religious practices, his refusal to deal with subjugated princes who were impure ('they were uncircumcised and ate fish') have been related in very classical and solemn language' (J. A. Wilson, *op. cit.*). So there is a surprising contrast 'between the puritan and retrograde mentality of the conqueror (the Sudano-Ethiopian culture tried to copy the earlier Egyptian civilisation and its religious conservatism verged on fanaticism) and the decadent mentality of the conquered' (Wilson, *ibidem*).

When victory was his, Piankhi, strangely enough, returned to his capital of Napata. Was he going to leave a viceroy behind to represent him? Egypt governed by an official dependent on the Nubian king, that would have been a comical state of affairs! But Piankhi was prudent; an official as high as that would have been able to make himself independent. It was better to control Egypt by using the oracles of Amun. Since they had been abused by the High Priests, the oracles were delivered at Thebes by a female 'Divine Adoratrice'. Piankhi made use of a trick: he forced the 'Divine Adoratrice' in office to choose his own sister, Amenirdis I, as her heir. Thus there was a member of his family at Thebes who would not abuse his confidence and would serve his plans. This was adding further to the humbling of Egypt, henceforth subject to the religious (and political) authority of a woman!

The 25th Nubian dynasty, commonly known as 'Kushite' or 'Ethiopian', remained in power from –751 to –656 and for more than a century its kings gave proof of administrative qualities often enough for Egypt to profit by their usurpation. They paid particular attention to the Thebaid. On the other hand, they were unable to master the anarchy fomented by the rivalries of the dynasts in the delta. As for the pious Taharqa, one of Piankhi's sons, he had to face the most formidable enemy. In –671 the Assyrians marched, crossed the Sinai desert, entered the delta (where the dynasts surrendered in cowardly fashion), arrived before Memphis and besieged and took the town. The fierce combat, sometimes in favour of the Nubian chiefs, took a decisive turn when the Assyrian army was commanded by Assurbanipal himself. Taharqa's successor, pursued as far as Thebes, which was sacked, had to flee to Upper Nubia and take refuge at Napata. Such are the vicissitudes of fortune.

Remote though it was, this retreat did not shelter the Nubians from raids. They were not conducted by the Assyrians, but by the Egyptians. Freed from the invaders by Psammetichus I, first king of the Saite period (–663–525), Egypt decided to make an end of the peril represented by the kingdom of Kush in the south. Less cautious in his movements than his predecessors, king of a country which was rediscovering its energy, Psammetichus II, on hearing about preparations by the Nubians to attack Egypt again, ascended the river to the First Cataract and from there hurled his armies southwards. They penetrated as far as the Third Cataract. Kush was conquered and its military power destroyed. Then the Pharaoh tried to wipe out the very memory of Nubian domination of Egypt, so that the opprobrium would disappear. He ordered that the names of the Nubian kings should be chiselled off all the temples and monuments. As we know, effacing a name in ancient Egypt was to reduce its bearer to nothingness.

12 ▸

◂ 13

14

However the loss of Egypt and the inroads of Psammetichus II's troops were unable to destroy the kingdom of Kush. Its kings continued to bear the title of 'Lords of the Two Lands', which shows that they did not despair of reconquering the north. On the other hand, the enterprise of the Saite Pharaoh drove them to turn southwards first. Napata, capital of the first kingdom, remained an important town and a market for the rich pasturelands of Dongola, but it soon abandoned this role to Meroë which became the definitive capital. Situated between the Fifth and the Sixth Cataracts Meroë was close to the track which enabled the caravans to reach Napata by land, so avoiding the impracticable rapids of the Fifth Cataract and cutting across the desert, thanks to the watering point at Jakdul, without following the irksome bend of the Nile to the east. Moreover Meroë possessed iron ore. Taharqa had the arms necessary for his struggle against the Assyrian forged there.
The civilisation of Meroë, at first purely copied from Egypt, finally became debased. Local elements merged with the pharaonic style; the Nubian penchant for massively heavy statuary was accentuated. Hieroglyphs were supplanted by a cursive script. A Meroitic culture was formed which was a curious amalgamation.
The kings of Kush have left us groups of funerary pyramids near Napata and Meroë. The monuments of these necropolises, with their chapel on one of the faces, and narrower silhouettes than their illustrious models, remind us of the pyramidions of the Thebaid. It has been suggested that Piankhi, on his return to his native land, ordered the builders to construct royal tombs similar to the pyramids at Giza and Saqqâra, a spectacle which had doubtless impressed him. Then his successors imitated him.
This conjecture does not satisfy all the archaeologists. The Meroitic tombs differ from the Egyptian ones. They stand out against the horizon, it is usually said, like serrations. They are acute, just as the hieroglyph representing the pyramid or the tomb is acute. Now this hieroglyph is anterior to the construction of the pharaonic edifices and this observation leads certain scholars to an unusual theory: the pyramid was not the invention of Egypt, but an imitation by her of African monuments. That would be one more argument for scholars who think that Egyptian civilisation is largely made up of African contributions.

Under the two Persian dominations, (–525 –404; –341–333), it does not seem as if the land of Kush had to suffer much from the new invader of Egypt. Herodotus, it is true, speaks of an expedition by Cambyses (–525–522) to 'Ethiopia', but there is no proof to guarantee it[1]. The Greek historian also tells us that the same Persian sovereign sent spies to Meroë. Under the pretext of offering gifts to the Kushite king their mission was to bring back information. Cambyses was curious to know if a vast altar consecrated to the Sun really existed close to the town. The spies found it, or rather saw a field covered with the most varied victuals which the inhabitants could consume freely. Magistrates must have supervised the provisioning of the place. The food was put down during the night, in secret, but a legend assured that it came spontaneously and the people of the country did not doubt that it was a gift of the earth.
If the kingdom of Kush had few relations and contacts with Persian Egypt, we would like to believe that it was in closer touch with the Macedonian and Ptolemaic dynasty in the Greek period. Doubtless the Kushites prudently tried to work northwards. They had good reasons, all commercial: iron, cattle, the products of Negro Africa in particular, wild beasts, feathers, ivory and

[1] Undoubtedly Cambyses did not get beyond Ibrim in Lower Nubia. According to certain chronicles, he destroyed Aswan and ravaged Philae.

pygmies, whom the Greeks of Egypt liked to use as servants or buffoons, formed considerable export products. However relations were often difficult: a conflict broke out between King Ergamenes of Kush (–225 –200) and Ptolemy V.

The Roman domination, as from –30, worried the Kushites even more. After the fall of the Ptolemies, they took strategic points in Lower Nubia. This success encouraged them. They were bold enough to descend to the Second Cataract. The queen (the 'Candace') Amanis Shaktete and her 30,000 Ethiopians took Philae, Syene and Elephantine, devastated the three towns and seized considerable booty in which figured the imperial statues, the supreme outrage.

Rome could not accept such a defeat. The prefect Petronius, at the head of shock troops, conquered the queen at Pselkis, routed her at Primis, pursued his advance to the Fourth Cataract and destroyed Napata and the famous temple of Amun at Gebel Barkal. True, Meroë, protected by its situation further south, escaped disaster and still remained a flourishing city, but the kingdom of Kush soon experienced a progressive decadence. The exploits of its ancient kings were for long extinguished in the indifference of history.

While Upper Nubia was fighting for survival and establishing itself as a kingdom, Lower Nubia – the Wawat of the Pharaohs, between the First and the Second Cataracts – mostly fell into utter neglect. However Psammetichus I brought the valley as far as the environs of Dakka under Egyptian dominion. This step was intended to help security. The same policy was pursued during the Greek period. The Ptolemies maintained themselves upstream from Aswan over a distance of 12 schoine, hence the name Dodekaschoinos (a schoinos equals 10 km or about 6 miles) given to this province. They built and rebuilt temples there, and installed garrisons. Beyond this Graeco-Egyptian zone, a territory under surveillance extended, and farther on began the disturbing land of Kush.

When the Romans became masters of Egypt, they relieved the Dodekaschoinos. They turned it into a rampart of Upper Egypt. However they had fixed their true frontier at Syene and Elephantine (Aswan). Did guarding this Nubian vestibule weigh on them? It seems that they fairly quickly considered the sacrifices and responsibilities it required to be out of proportion. Masters of North Africa, they received the products of Central Africa by caravans which traversed the Sahara. Thus Nubia lost its importance, it was no longer the only transit route.

Other dangers persisted. Raids by the nomads were frequent, especially by the Blemmyes, formidable looters whose existence had already been mentioned by Strabo. The Blemmyes, affected by the influence of Egyptian cults, worshipped Isis. In order to avoid conflicts, they had to be admitted to Philae and even, for part of the year, authorised to take home with them statues of the goddess. In spite of the troops garrisoned at Primis, Pselkis, Kerkis, Talmis and Taphis, the audacity of these bands did not lessen. They even penetrated into the Thebaid. The Roman empire, which was already experiencing the first signs of decline, could not allow itself to expend too much strength on such a remote frontier, nor could it expose itself to the risks of abandoning it. At the end of the third century, Diocletian solved the problem. He decided to entrust the guardianship of these territories to a local tribe, the Nobatae. He recalled his troops at Syene and Elephantine. In fact the Dodekaschoinos belonged to the Nobatae and Blemmyes.

Nubia was going to emerge from antiquity in its turn. In 379, the edict of Theodosius the Great proclaimed Christianity the official

religion of Egypt. So Nubia was linked with the world of the new faith.
A vast drive to convert the people took place there. Sent by Byzantium, Julian, undoubtedly the first of the missionaries, did not hesitate to preach the gospel to these Nobatae who were reputed to be formidable, to the peoples in the regions of the Second Cataract and even to those who lived beyond. It seems that he was quite well received, as was Theodorus, bishop of Philae, who accompanied him. But the task was arduous, for these Egyptianised peoples primarily intended to remain faithful to the beliefs of Egypt.
Christianity, however, was implanted and took root. A number of the faithful, formerly persecuted in the north, had sought refuge in the Nubian lands in the south and thus prepared them to receive a new teaching.
These believers often excited sympathy by the example of a life of humility, sacrifice and devotion to travellers and their fellow man. Those who were called the 'Desert fathers' aroused attention and interest. In short, evangelisation was rapid, as the establishment of large Christian kingdoms, from the middle of the sixth century onwards, bears witness. One of them, Nobatia, extended from the First to the Second Cataract, then passed this limit to reach Makuria, which itself stretched to the south of the ancient Meroë. Further south, the kingdom of Alodia reached the regions where the White Nile and the Blue Nile join.
Professor L. P. Kirwan, director of the Royal Geographic Society of London, has rightly insisted on the importance of these Christian centuries in Nubia. He praises them in these words: 'During this period, Nubia was a very prosperous and powerful country. On both banks of the Nile many towns, churches and flourishing monasteries succeeded each other. Church and State were remarkably organised, largely on the Byzantine model. Rarely, in the course of the long history of the Nubian people, did it attain by its architecture, its art, its civil and military organisation and the awakening of a national consciousness a degree of civilisation as high as in this golden age of Christian Nubia.'
These little Christian states of Nubia showed a remarkable longevity. Some of them lasted until the beginning of the fourteenth century; Egypt, Moslem since the year 20 of the Hegira, i.e. for seven centuries, had not conquered them at this date. For seven centuries they compelled the respect of their Moslem neighbours and were opposed, by their very existence, to the expansion of Islam towards negro Africa.
In 1173 the Sheikh Shams ed Daulah, father of the illustrious Sultan Saladin, took the important city of Ibrim, destroyed it and transformed the church into a mosque. From then on Christianity could not help growing weaker in Nubia, often menaced by its own undertakings and divisions. Its last king, Kerenbes, was deported to Cairo in 1315. Nubia was almost wholly converted to Islam, but Upper Nubia again played its traditional role as a refuge: Christian communities established themselves there.

5

Horeau, a ninteenth-century artist, drew for our enjoyment an isometric view of Nubia around 1835, in which romanticism gently woos an anxiety to leave nothing out. The artist, as was right, has placed himself on a sheer peak in the centre of the composition – at least I imagine that the meditative silhouette on the summit is his. At the foot of the rock his escort awaits him, with horses and dromedaries. Did M. Horeau really come this far? I do not know, but I would like to think so. Below, on the right he has depicted the islets of the Second Cataract: they are

15

like a flock of sheep in a hurry to cross the stream, their necks out of the water, foam springing up from their passage. Wise palm trees like the feather dusters of good housekeepers await them on the other bank. There are also the feluccas with white sails which go so well with the landscape.

From his promontory M. Horeau sees the Nile – and shows it to us – winding away to the very distant distances. The meanders cease when the upper edge of the picture is reached – if the paper had been bigger we should have been taken to the sea! We must not complain; this visual promenade offers us an itinerary downstream from Buhen (not depicted) to Philae and even a little beyond. Our eye wanders from temple to temple in this landscape – which might have been the work of a naive and archaeologically-minded Patinir. From the two sanctuaries of Abu Simbel and the cliff of Ibrim, M. Horeau has depicted the monuments as a painter of battles depicts the corps of an army. M. Horeau must have been happy on his rock. From the banks of the valley forty centuries contemplated him – and he contemplated them. What merits this 'aerial' view has! A map indicating the sites would stir imagination less. A series of photographs would not give the same feelings of a marvellous panorama. Through this drawing, before lingering among the details, we have a global vision of Nubia with all its riches united. Here it appears to us, to use the expression of an archaeologist who has a gift for happy phrases, as 'the greatest open-air museum in the world' (Desroches-Noblecourt).

For months, from the time the construction of the Sadd el Aali was decided on, we have believed this museum condemned.

This is what is going to disappear, we said, and we looked at the picture: the artless perspective summed up the monuments which were doomed to disappear beneath the waters. Even M. Horeau was unable to see or show everything, his description needed completing. Among the islets of the Second Cataract which the drawer is contemplating, there is one, that of Shahgil, where the remains of a neolithic fishing place have been discovered. Six or seven thousand years ago fishermen came there to dry and smoke their fish: 'The sand covers fish skeletons mixed with fragments of pottery to a depth of some eight inches, below which there is a deep layer of sand. The fish must have been of a good size and similar to the big perch which are found in the Nile today'.[1] Further on, on the island of Uronarti, a stone age workshop has been revealed. Of course, traces of prehistoric man are not found in this region alone. The ancient terraces of the river contain many. On the heights dominating Abu Simbel, more Stone Age remains show the antiquity of the population of this place which normally only recalls Ramesses II and Queen Nefertari. There is no shortage of rock engravings. On a rocky wall almost adjoining the temple of Wadi Es Sebui, a fawn gallops with a giraffe and an elephant, a small exotic zoo, which one would seek in vain on the present-day banks of the river, climatic conditions having changed since the age when these silhouettes were drawn by a prehistoric man.

So the water was going to drown these sites which were still not nearly catalogued, although they were rich in information about our most remote ancestors. Had the excavations adequately covered the Egyptian period at least? One noticed that several sites still called for the labour of archaeologists and ethnologists and that they would suffer the common fate. Necropolises and cities still guarded secrets, perhaps even remarkable objects and works of art.

It was relatively simple to make an inventory of the monuments. They were grouped by periods. The citadels of the Second Cataract belonged to the most ancient period: Buhen, Aksha, Mirgissa, Semna and Kumma. Then came the works of the New Kingdom: Amada, admirable temple of the 18th dynasty, preceded the later sanctuaries, nearly all hollowed out of the rock (speos or hemispeos): Beit el Wali, Gerf Hussein, Wadi Es Sebui, Derr, Ellesyia, the chapel of Pennut at Aniba, Ibrim, Abu Oda and Gebel Chams, the whole dominated by the two temples of Abu Simbel.

The temples of the Graeco-Roman period, often established on the foundations of earlier edifices, are situated at intervals upstream from Philae, without going far beyond the boundaries of the Dodekaschoinos: Debod, Kertassi, Taffa, Kalabsha, Dendur, Dakka and Maharraqah.

Christian Nubia was not forgotten. Not only had antique monuments been transformed into churches (they contained Christian symbols united with those of pharaonic Egypt), but civil and religious buildings, frescoes and written documents were also revealed to us by the excavations at Ikhmindi, Ibrim and Faras. Proofs of the importance of a little known period and its art multiplied.

Obvious riches. Riches to be discovered. M. Horeau's picture needed enlarging. The open-air museum had its 'reserves'. A more complete inventory resulted from the peril.

[1] Cf.: R. Keating, *Un Passé inconnu surgit des sables* (Courrier de l'Unesco, Nov. 1962).

It is not the purpose of this book to relate in detail how it was averted. If the construction of the Sadd el Aali required constant efforts, the safeguarding of the monuments of Nubia required an equal perseverance. There was the mobilisation of goodwill to ensure the survival of the archaeological treasures as there was to ensure the daily life of the Egyptians. The task proved complicated. Its various aspects escaped no one. First of all it was necessary to establish an exhaustive documentation, so that the threatened patrimony was caught in images for ever: by technical photography, by epigraphic abstracts, by the processes of photogrammetry which translated the relief of buildings and statuary into contour lines and thus made accurate reproductions possible. Then urgent excavation work was needed: finishing off excavations which were in progress and starting them on new ground. Aerial photographs facilitated the establishment of a map of sites.

The most important thing remained: the rescue of the monuments themselves. It was decided that the majority would be dismantled, 'cut up' into sections, or extracted from the rock, in the case of the speos, and transported to safety, then reassembled and reconstructed on new sites – in Nubia for preference. However this solution could not be applied to the two groups of monuments – the most important and the most valuable – at Philae and Abu Simbel. Enormous though the enterprise might seem, their preservation *in situ* was envisaged, on the very spot where they stood. Philae would be protected by a belt of dams and rocks, Abu Simbel would rise above the level of the future reservoir. We shall examine these solutions in the chapters devoted to the different buildings – and we asked an expert, Mr. Colonetti, to expound the methods of preservation adopted for the speos of Abu Simbel.

Such an entreprise was beyond the powers of the United Arab Republic and the Republic of the Sudan.[1] It required international collaboration. It fell to Unesco to call on the world to unite in saving this common spiritual treasure. On 8 March 1960, Mr. Vittorino Veronese, Director General of the Organisation, launched a solemn appeal so that 'from a land which throughout the centuries has been the scene of – or the stake in – so many covetous disputes should spring a convincing proof of international solidarity.' M. André Malraux, French Minister for Cultural Affaires, said in his reply: 'At the moment when our civilisation divines a mysterious transcendence in art and one of the still obscure sources of its unity, at the moment when we are bringing into a single family relationship the masterpieces of so many civilisations which knew nothing of or even hated each other, you are proposing an action which brings all men together to defy the forces of dissolution.' When he was assured that the most imposing of the sanctuaries would not be lost beneath the waters M. René Maheu, the new director of Unesco, could say: 'The rescue of Abu Simbel is a spiritual act.'

[1] In recognition of the aid granted by foreign nations, the Government of the U.A.R. offered: *a)* to cede to parties which have carried out excavations in Nubia at least half the proceeds of their finds, with the exception of certain unique pieces, which will remain the property of the Egyptian State, in conformity with the international regulation in force in this domain; *b)* to authorise these same parties to make excavations in other parts of Egypt not at present forming part of recognised concessions, the proceeds of the excavations being divided on the same principles; *c)* to cede certain of the monuments doomed to disappear, with a view to their transfer abroad; *d)* to cede, in recognition of international action, statues, steles, inscriptions and other archaeological objects taken from the collections and reserves of the State. – The Government of the Sudan recalled that by the terms of its national legislation foreign missions authorised to excavate were entitled to half the proceeds of their excavations, with the exception of *unica*.
Cf.: *Documents d'Information,* Unesco, 1960-1964.

These last words were spoken in November 1963. They marked the outcome of untold devotion. Since we were privileged to go to Abu Simbel at the beginning of the rescue work and later, when they had acquired their full importance, how can we help witnessing to what was accomplished? If it is right to recall 'the faith which moves mountains', the expression should be understood both literally and figuratively, since it was a question of raising the mountain of the temple! The bank and the square, the halls of the sanctuary, which we had known almost deserted and favourable to meditation, were thronged with architects, photographers, specialists in photogrammetry, epigraphists, archaeologists, historians, quantity-surveyors, technicians of all the disciplines concerned, qualified workmen, navvies, cinema and television cameramen and I don't know who else. If you wanted to look at some bas-relief again, you no longer found it in the shade which once added to its mysterious beauty, projectors flooded it with light for the needs of scientific photographers – and the operators were astonished at your preference for those you had taken once as it were by torchlight, in a sacred twilight. You were asked to climb scaffoldings so that your photograph would suffer no distortion of perspective; in vain you protested about your liking for 'natural' perspectives, for views taken at a man's height. This was because to many of the men working here (in heat often higher than 104°F) fell the task of leaving an exact 'recording' of the monument if it happened not to be saved. At the same time, in case the necessary funds should be obtained, groups of engineers studied the possibilities of cutting up and lifting the whole block. Sometimes doubts arose: would they manage to protect the temple? To regain confidence, it was enough to listen to Mme Christiane Desroches-Noblecourt. This Egyptologist was the soul of the defence in France; rarely, I confess, did passion and erudition seem to fuse so closely. How many languages were spoken at Abu Simbel? For our part, we heard (apart from Arabic) English, German, French, Spanish, Italian, Swedish and Polish.

Doubtless it was natural for the scholars to defend the object of their studies in this way, but the emotion aroused by the submersion (then thought probable) of the remains of ancient Nubia also conquered a large lay public and aroused the anxious attention of those interested in art and history, all the more so as Egypt of the Pharaohs exercises an attraction close to fascination on many people. Perhaps we may be allowed to bear personal witness again. In 1960 we shot a film devoted to the monuments in peril for Unesco and French television, putting our meagre store of knowledge and, as they say, all our hearts into it. We do not know what results it had abroad. On the other hand we know the effect it produced in France. We immediately received a flood of mail. In their letters, viewers of all classes asked us how to act, how to help the rescue operation. Some of them proposed opening a subscription list, ready themselves to contribute their obol. Others – the young, students in particular – offered to go and work in Nubia at their own expense during their holidays. It appears that movements like this from generous motives should be put down to the credit of our age.

It is true that one met a more lukewarm attitude in certain 'authorised' circles. Egypt, one heard, is rich enough in wonders, it can do without the Nubian ones. Did the monuments themselves merit considerable sums being spent to protect them? Some people claimed that they were being too highly honoured. After all, they said, many temples were copies from the Graeco-Roman period. As for the two sanctuaries of Abu Simbel, objects of the deepest concern, they had their denigrators: to believe them, they only witnessed to a megalomaniac king's bad taste for the colossal. How many times have we not thought of Flaubert's comic phrase on seeing the four colossi of Ramesses: 'Beautiful heads... Nasty feet!' The great writer had these moods.[1] Doubtless it escaped him that the feet and legs together were conceived as a base which had to be massive to support the broad torso, symbol of strength which in its turn supported the smiling and serene face: the colossi seem to obey a movement of elevation, a sort of ascension of thick and corporal matter towards serenity, wisdom and spirit. In the same way, the hollowing out of the temple in the sandstone and the interior dimensions it was given, were not merely a technical tour de force. Ramesses' architects could easily have built a temple in the open air here. They wanted the sanctuary to be in the rock, as if *in the womb of the other world.*

At the time these words are written, what could be saved is saved (or will be). However there is no guarantee that the threats have ceased. Setting aside even the possibility of accident which could occur during the reconstruction of buildings of fragile stone, another danger hangs over them. The stones are saved, but on what sites will the monuments be re-assembled? To worry about this is not to call in question the skill of the reconstructors – and, in any case, there was no remedy save displacement, erection on a new site. Should this site be Nubian, or above the preceding one, we shall have 'displaced' monuments, using the adjective in the sense given it when designating the victims of a contemporary tragedy: the displaced persons, the DP's. Can we imagine, for example, the cathedral of Notre Dame de Paris cut up into pieces and then rebuilt on the heights of Montmartre or Mont-Valérien, or even the Montagne Sainte-Geneviève? It would miss the two arms of the Seine to embrace its island, its chosen situation in the heart of a landscape.

May we not fear that the temples of Nubia will feel the lack of the natural surroundings which contributed to the personality of each one of them? Philae, admittedly, will be an island again for the twelve months of the year – but in a vast basin, away from the river whose current will no longer flow towards it from the south, as the myth required. One will reply that from the beginning of the century the monuments no longer looked as they once had, since the water accumulated by the old dam already reduced the bank, reached them and hid some of them for nine months. This is true. But there was Nubia, its people, its houses, its villages, its harsh steep banks. There was what remained of the water and land route, once followed by conquerors and conquered, the long vein of a flux and reflux, the long corridor of fruitful exchanges between north and south. Lost Nubia was what the rescued monuments of Nubia would lack.

In this book we have not merely tried to show the works in their intrinsic beauty, we have always tried to situate them in the place which they occupied during the centuries. We have described them as a traveller could see them before the submersion of the banks they adorned. It seemed to us that witness should be borne to what Nubia was, cramped between the river and the deserts. May these pages bear worthy witness to this human adventure: the birth, growth and decadence of a civilisation. Yet a civilisation which is not disappearing: its stones, its images save it.

[1] The great writer, whose *Voyages* are a model of freedom of vision, sometimes had his moods! Let us quote these reflections which were actually made about Abu Simbel: 'The Egyptian temples bore me to distraction. Is this going to become like the churches in Brittany, like the waterfalls in the Pyrenees? O necessity! Doing what it is necessary to do; being always, depending on the circumstances (and although the repugnance of the moment puts you off), like a young man, a traveller, an artist, a son, a citizen etc., should be.' Gustave Flaubert's journey in Egypt took place from 1849 to 1850.

Prehistoric Nubia, pharaonic Nubia, Nubia of the Greek period, Roman Nubia, Christian Nubia, Islamic Nubia ... The profile we have sketched is inseparable from the winding line drawn by a long stretch of the river, and now we see it, on the same stretch, waiting to become a new destiny for men.

For millennia peoples have lived on the two Nubian banks, leaving there the proofs of what they were and what they did. Columns testifying to their beliefs or simple engraved stones, the defence walls of their ridiculous quarrels or the colossi of their masters – continous alluvial deposits like those of the Nile. The Egyptian sign of life and the Christian cross, the Roman ensign and the Moslem crescent have succeeded each other in this landscape which for so long now has presented a truly surrealist vision: a river flowing in the desert and, with scanty crops barely separating the lip to lip of sand and water, the almost too obvious symbol of death and life lip to lip.

Shall we call the men who populated Nubia strangers, unknown? We do not know them only from having seen the Nubians of our day perform gestures similar to those they performed down the centuries: the same movement to lift the balancing pole of a well, to shift a sail when tacking from one bank to the other, to push a seed into the mud. We have a more inward knowledge of them, independent of circumstances. We know them, we recognise them. To rejoin them through their works of art is not to succumb to archaeology, but to approach their still living truth. In the course of time they have tried, as we all try, to leave behind them not only a memory, but a trace. Could we have abandoned that trace to destruction unless we accepted that our own might disappear in its turn? We are accountable for the past, as for the present and the future. A great people of today needs bread. The great peoples of yesterday need those victors over the tomb and oblivion: stones, assembled, sculptured and storied stones. Yes, if we had to choose between bread and stones for present-day Egypt, without being allowed to dodge the dilemma, we would have chosen bread, if it were only in memory of a dead fellah upstream from Asyut, one evening when the flood came unexpectedly.

In truth there was no dilemma. To say 'bread *or* stones' was to doubt, to renounce. We had to say 'bread *and* stones' – and we did so. A *conjunction* took the place of an adverb and honour was saved, that honour which knows that Man creates man, but only by being faithful to the continuity in which the past is united with the present, and the future.

Philae

◄ 18

19

21 ►

20

22

23

Philae... At the beginning of this century these two syllables were enough to wound cultivated minds and sensitive souls.
For many people the name summed up the contempt of modern times for the past, the peril with which 'progress' threatened civilisation.
Engineers had built a dam at Aswan in Egypt near the banks of the First Cataract where the soldiers of General Bonaparte once established their last bivouac, in spite of the threat of the Mamelukes. Beneath the sheet of water thus held back, a sacred tablet would disappear: the island of Philae, on which stood not fragmentary remains, but solid proofs of antique grandeur – preserved for more than two thousand years.
Soon water was going to drown temples, sanctuaries, porticoes, the images and symbols of a secret. A place of ancient mystery would be destroyed at a time when Europe was losing interest in her own spiritual mysteries. The Aswan dam was like the line we draw under a column of figures. The adding up had to be done. The total would represent the classical culture in which pharaonic Egypt had played its part. This total then had to be included in the new synthesis made necessary by the discovery of the 'barbarian' cultures and the scientific inventions of this century. When Philae went under, the idols of Oceania would already be installed, African statues and masks would already be claiming our attention, modifying our vision and awaiting their transposition into Western aesthetics.

On the plane of art alone, not to mention the sciences and the change in scientific thinking, knowledge felt cramped within the bounds of the traditional 'humanities'. *The Death of Philae* (by Pierre Loti) had the value of a symbol or a premonitory sign. Admittedly no one had yet told civilisations that they were mortal, but in a confused way they were afraid of learning that they were. The submersion of a few temples made Europe aware of what was foretold in the depths: a new cultural crisis. New, yes, but similar to those which the old continent has suffered every time that it has had both to preserve the heritage of the past and unite this heritage with the disturbing windfall of unforeseen heritages.

Long after the construction of the dam, about 1923, when I was a child, I sometimes heard the name of Philae skimming like a pebble on the calm waters of family conversations. My parents did not know Egypt. They can only have had a very vague idea of the temples of the sacred island, but Pierre Loti was one of their favourite authors and he had just protested against the iconoclasm of the builders of the reservoir. On the lips of my family Philae was associated with other names which witnessed to contemporary philistinism. The inundation of its masterpieces joined company with the burning of the library of Louvaine and the bombardment of Paris by 'Big Bertha'. These events together constituted the unatonable, original sin of the century.

One day my father read aloud to me long passages from the last chapter of *Le Mort de Philae* (The Death of Philae). I was impressed by the story of the boat trip the writer took at night in the actual interior of the half-flooded temple, in the hypostyle halls. When he evoked the sound of ancient sculptured stones detaching themselves from the walls and falling into the dark water I was as if transported into a world where everything beautiful was flowing into oblivion. My father paused, I remember. He was dreaming, too. 'There can be nothing left now,' he said sadly.

He went on reading. We returned to the bank with Loti, we entered the café of the 'horrible village' of Shellal: 'This desert tavern stinks of absinthe. It is heated by a *brasero*. It was hurriedly built out of tin cans and broken whisky cases . . . ' The enchantment stopped. It was impossible to make a better contrast between the grandeur of the past and the poverty of the present.

There was another poverty. That of the people who lived on the banks of the Nile. The project of the first dam had been established not to suppress, but to alleviate it. The disease of a poor country had to be treated, as the disease of an incurable patient is treated, by 'prolonging' it. Many well-disposed people could not accept the proposition: in their eyes the humanitarian aim of the project was hypocritical. The increase in cultivable land would make larger cotton crops possible. But would the fellaheen of Egypt profit by them? Very little. On the contrary, the real beneficiaries would be the big Manchester cotton spinners. People recognised the self-interested policy of perfidious Albion – and it was easy to recognise it, because it was obvious. Tenacious Anglophobia in France provided arms for the defenders of Philae; barely four years had elapsed since the humiliation of Fashoda . . . Protests by scholars, men of learning and amateur enthusiasts were so animated that the initial project had to be modified in 1902. The waters would not rise as high as had been planned. Culture had won a point.

The dam also had its fanatics. Voices were raised in the other camp. One of them had a strange ring which was to be heard again in the history of the century: 'This offering of millions of cubic feet of water to the goddess Hathor by the enlightened minds of the West is the cruellest, most dangerous and most senseless sacrifice which has ever been made on the altar of a false religion. Let Egypt struggle without hope and let its people die of hunger, so long as the professors rejoice and the tourists can carve their names on ancient stones!' These sarcastic remarks caused a scandal. They were made by an Englishman, of course. His name was repeated with reprobation. It was Winston Churchill.

Nonetheless the fate of Philae was decided. The dam was built from 1907 to 1912, then from 1932 to 1934. Since the beginning of the century, water covers the monuments during the nine months of the year when it accumulates, and exposes them when the opening of the sluices allows it to spread and circulate the alluvial deposits of the 'fertile floods' over Egypt. Philae, however, has not disappeared. Its stones have not fallen into the river one by one and the current has not carried them away, as Loti feared. True, its polychrome paintings, which nineteenth-century travellers reported as still very bright, are no more. On the other hand, the annual immersions have prevented the monuments from being rasped, emerypapered by the sand carried by the desert winds, especially the fierce khamsin. The stone does not exude the corrosive salt which passes through its pores from the soil by a sort of osmosis in other parts of Egypt.

Philae is not dead. The site of a divine epiphany, it is an epiphany in itself, every year.

2

It is possibly one of the misfortunes of our civilisation that we can no longer see anything without having seen it already.
The explosive impact of a work of art inside us, the blinding flash of its first appearance, the sudden awakening which results from it: we are always deprived of these emotions beforehand by modern techniques. They accustom us to Mozart and Van Gogh, as they do to atomic fission. There are stock-piles of sound – and just as many visual stock-piles. We are in advance of ourselves. We long for surprise. Nowadays we are told what we are going to experience.
Is it still possible for a traveller to come upon Philae unawares? He prepares himself not so much to get to know as to recognise and verify. Forms and shapes slumber in the chaotic loess of images deposited, among impersonal memories, between conscious knowledge and the idleness of dreams. For a long time now the itineraries of 'organised tours' (one of today's horrible expressions) make Philae the limit of their last lap southward. It is the suburb of Aswan. From the dam you can see Philae, and from Philae the dam. Nubia the easy way.
Fortunately the island is protected by the heat and by the water. It does not emerge until August. It has already begun to submerge towards the middle of October. It needs the torrid light to expose itself. Then you can land on the shore of the amphibious island, cross the dried cracked mud, walk beneath its porticoes into the courtyards and the sanctuaries.
In these baking months tourists are rare or in a hurry to get back to the fans of the Aswan hotels and the enticing sound of ice cubes tinkling in their glasses. Only the devotees, the enthusiasts, the worshippers, remain, those who hear the sistra shaking in honour of Hathor in the fiery heat.
For most of the year you can only see the two summits of the great pylon of Isis. Two stone tables, like flat tombstones, lie strangely on the shapeless water, the water like that of the Ocean from which, according to the cosmogony of Heliopolis, the Sun, 'that which exists by itself', was born. The feluccas of the Nile, warned by the buoys and the agitation of the waves, skirt the sunken massif. One dreams of some impossible walk under the water, of the apparition among the eddies of tall figures perpetuating the offerings. Philae encourages delirium.
The tales of the travellers who knew it before the construction of the first dam, the surveys and drawings they have left us (how can we help admiring the engravings in the *Description de l'Egypte*, published in Paris in 1820?), the photographs taken before the

work done in 1899, they all combine to give a different picture. Vegetation covered the island. Palm trees, acacias and briars were intermingled with the stones. There was a direct relationship between the fanning out of the palms and the floral exuberance of certain capitals. Sloping tree trunks emphasised the uprightness of the columns. The yards of many sailing boats moored alongside the shore seemed to spring from the undergrowth. Looking at old albums we can better understand the enthusiasm of the visitors and their use of this hyperbole: 'The Nile makes a detour as if it came to seek out and encompass this enchanted isle...' These are the least inflated words used by Vivant-Denon in his *Voyage dans la Basse et la Haute-Egypte pendant les campagnes du général Bonaparte,* published in 1802. Philae appeared like some Cythera entirely surrounded by deserts to these travellers of the last century. 24

The charm of the island was all the greater because to reach it the visitor had to pass through a bristling, megalithic, wild scenery. A kind of battlefield.

13 It was the Nile which had fought the battle. The accumulated blocks of stone show its relentless persistence in wearing away, dislocating and breaking the ridge which opposed its advance. The main features of the cataract are rounded polished masses which look like pachyderms swimming. But upstream the scenery is different. Accumulations of rock interrupt the surface of the river, rising in strange formations like towers and ruined fortresses. The islands seem to result from the suddenly halted clash of giant boulders. Stone surmounts stone. These piles look like a chaotic quarry in which we recognise or invent shapes. We can imagine that we see effigies eroded by the centuries. Before arriving at Philae you pass rocks with a Victor Hugo-ish eloquence – and perhaps at dawn they resound as the colossi of Memnon resounded? Sometimes the profile is imperious, the stature pharaonic. It is a challenge to the imagination. This natural chaos evokes a battle of the giants, but sometimes also the assembly of ancient kings, the council of a prince on his throne. There is no doubt, that is Pharaoh in profile. Elsewhere amorphous brutes... The adoration of baetyls becomes understandable here. There is an energy in this accumulated mass of eloquent, upright and toppling stones.

The ancient Egyptians, observant as they were, were well aware that the river came from beyond Philae, from the south. Nevertheless they situated in these regions the two rocks Môphi and Krôphi between which, according to them, the Nile emerged from a pit. These wild surroundings must once have contrasted with the shady elegance of the island, enhancing the value of a pleasant oasis. Today, in the centre of an austere cirque which is only slightly relieved by distant sand-dunes, it is no longer fanned by palm trees. When it reappears, there is nothing but mud on the ground, but the mud soon produces a green mantle.

Then the soil wears the other colour of Osiris. It is the black god of the other world and of death, but also the green lord of rebirth.

3

Are we accepting an over-simplified analogy by linking the modern reappearances of Philae with the antique resurrection of the God? Here everything speaks of Osiris and his sister-bride Isis. We are in the domain of myth. The mind cannot escape it, and if it tried to do so would be the poorer for it. The time has come to cease being a traveller. Philae is barely separated from its neighbour Bigah by an arm of the Nile. There, in that granitic chaos, Osiris was buried after his disjointed limbs had been reassembled. The territory belonged to him personally and 29, 30, 31

24

no one was allowed to enter it except the priests in charge of the daily libations of milk. Every ten days the effigy of Isis left the temple of Philae on the sacred boat. The wife was visiting her husband. She attended the solemn offerings placed in the 365 bowls which surrounded the body, gifts for every day of the year. Thus Isis, she who nursed and preserved life on earth, visited the Lord of the dead and of eternal life. The union, the secret resemblance of the two lives was asserted by this navigation between two islands.

Hunting – *abaton* – was forbidden on the territory of Osiris. Fishing was only allowed away from the shore. All music was forbidden. It was a place of silence. An admirable conception of a sanctuary wholly devoted to the mystery of *waiting*.
It would not have been right for husband and wife to have been separated. Isis *lives* in her temple at Philae, but she reposes beside Osiris in the 'sacred plain' of the island, as a text of Diodorus Siculus tells us. A divine decree 'written by the god Thoth' can be read in Philae itself on the Roman gate named after the Emperor Hadrian, inside an aedicule which seems to have been a chapel of Osiris. The gods Re, Shu and Geb recognise the sovereignty of Isis and Osiris over 'the Holy Mound' (i.e. Bigah). All the details of the form of worship are given. It is worth quoting part of the text (in Etienne Drioton's translation): 'The Holy Mound' is the sacred golden territory of Osiris and his sister Isis. It was predestined for this from the beginning of the world... Milk will not lack for the Mound of the Sacred Wood nor for the temple where Osiris is buried. Let the divine service be held there every day by the high priest of the time and let a libation be made to Isis, lady of Philae, when the libation is poured there every day. No one must beat the tambourine there, nor play the harp or the flute. No man should ever enter there, nor should anyone, large or small, walk there. No bird shall be hunted there... None of those who shall be present shall raise his voice during the sacred period which Isis, lady of Philae, who is on the throne, shall spend there to make the libation every ten days. Isis, lady of Philae, shall embark for the Holy Mound on holidays, in the sacred boat...' The inscription is engraved on the gate built by a Roman Emperor who reigned from +117 to +138. It shows not only the persistence, but also the importance of the cult of Isis and Osiris in the second century of our era, at a time when Egypt had not been governed by indigenous dynasties for several centuries. We may ask ourselves the reasons for this continuity – and still more about its significance. This is the moment to reread Plutarch, who was in fact Hadrian's tutor. We are indebted to him for the most complete (and the most touched up!) history of Osiris. Everything began, if you like, at the level of the government of men. Osiris was a king who administered his kingdom wisely. This wisdom and the benefits which accrued from it aroused the wrath of his brother Seth. Seth hatched a dark plot to get rid of him. He invited him to a banquet. When the ceremony was drawing to a close, a coffin was brought which Seth had had built to the exact dimensions of his brother's body. Then the host asked each of his guests to lie down inside the box to see if any of them fitted it. Only Osiris did, but scarcely was he inside the box when the lid was closed on top of him. There was our wise sovereign caught like a rat in a trap. And the conspirators hastened to throw the coffin and its occupant into the Nile.
Then Isis's quest began. She sought the body of her husband. Nephthys, her sister, accompanied her, although she was the wife of Seth, the murderer! Conducted by Plutarch, we travel as far as Byblos in Phoenicia. The chest-coffin had reached there, but it had run against a tree whose trunk, in growing, had encircled it. Soon the tree acquired

such strength that the king of Byblos made it into the central pillar of his palace. Isis guessed where her beloved lay. She acquired such favour with the king that she was given the chest. She took it back to Egypt and hid it. The wicked Seth soon discovered the body. As we know, he cut it up into pieces and dispersed them throughout Egypt (according to other traditions he threw them into the Nile). Isis, still helped by Nephthys, tried to solve a divine jigsaw puzzle – if you will pardon the irreverence. For a long time she sought the scattered limbs and finally found them. Then she gathered them together and recomposed the body: in this way she 'invented' the first mummy, from then on the practice of embalming by the Egyptians would repeat the action of Isis. Another tradition tells us that the goddess turned herself into a bird. She flapped her wings above the body to reintroduce life-giving breath into it. She did not manage to revive it, but she did succeed in becoming pregnant. A miracle which was all the more remarkable because Osiris's penis was the only part of his body which could not be found. Three fish of the Nile had shared it, a barbel, a tiger-fish and an oxyrhynchus.

Horus, son of Osiris and Isis, was born. His mother brought him up in the marshes of the delta, protecting him from danger. He grew up. Soon he rallied his father's supporters and challenged Seth. The struggle was long, difficult and fierce, abounding in vicissitudes which Plutarch often omits. We see gods take the assassin's side – and even Isis has a singular partiality for him. Nevertheless Horus was victorious. He forced recognition of his father's rights and his own legitimacy.

Plutarch had travelled in Egypt. He heard different stories which he blended into his own narrative. Undoubtedly he added inventions of his own: the voyage to Byblos, for example, of which no trace is found elsewhere: and ignored other traditional episodes. His legend needs completing with the material provided by the texts of the pyramids and the tales of the New Kingdom, but that is quite outside our competence and it would take us far away from Philae . . . Let us return to the victorious Horus. We note that he did not re-establish his father on the earthly throne. He occupied it himself. However, the other world was the kingdom of Osiris. In this way a sort of friendly share-out between father and son was established. But the two powers were not separated. On the contrary, they were dependent on each other. The legend testifies to this: Osiris prepared Horus for the battle, he transmitted his power to him (his Ka, if you like). For his part Horus offered his father the eye he had lost in his fight against Seth and which he had managed to recover. These are images of mutual obligations. All the acts of Horus guarantee the divine nature of Osiris – and the divinity of Osiris in turn justifies the acts of Horus. They are indispensable to each other.

But Horus is Pharaoh. Son of the dead king, he is the living king who conquered Seth, the evil one. His divine father inspires him. Now he turns towards the sky and recognises in Re another self, and then he is designated to be the omnipotent intermediary between the divine energies and men: he unites in himself the sun of death and the sun of life. The character of Egyptian kingship cannot be fully understood without the myth of Osiris. Agricultural peoples often established a relationship between death and fertility. Apparently paradoxical, the two words even united in the single figure of a god who presided over both of them, lord of the tomb and the furrow. Osiris illustrated this identity in the exercise of a dual function. He was king of the underworld, but this death gave birth to Horus, just as the seed in dying gives birth to the plant. Fundamentally he was seed. His theophany was the plant which grows and blossoms, and returns to seed via flower and fruit. Thus he accomplished the complete cycle of life and death. By a natural

27

process, he was the guarantor of eternal life and of rebirth. He denied that death was an end, he ensured that it was a beginning or a new beginning. He actually contradicted the idea of nothingness, as the king whom his enemy could not destroy, through the medium of bodily disintegration.

A small building built under the Antonines stands at Philae on the west side of the temple of Isis, at the height of the second pylon. There is no doubt that it is a chapel consecrated to Osiris. The intermediate register on the north wall is decorated with a relief (unfortunately in bad condition) which illustrates what we have just said. To the left a rocky wall, formed of piled up blocks, recalls the scenery in the neighbourhood of the island. The base of this cliff is hollowed out into a cave whose entrance is formed by the body of a guardian serpent: the god Nile is seated on it. Outside, quite close, the cow-headed goddess Hathor is pouring the contents of a vase onto a base possibly representing an irrigation canal. Above the base, in a thick clump, are cereals. At the level of the ears a bird with a human head appears to walk: the traditional representation of the soul after death – and here it is the bird-soul of Osiris. On the other side four divinities succeed each other and perform

35

27

◂ 29

31

◂ 30

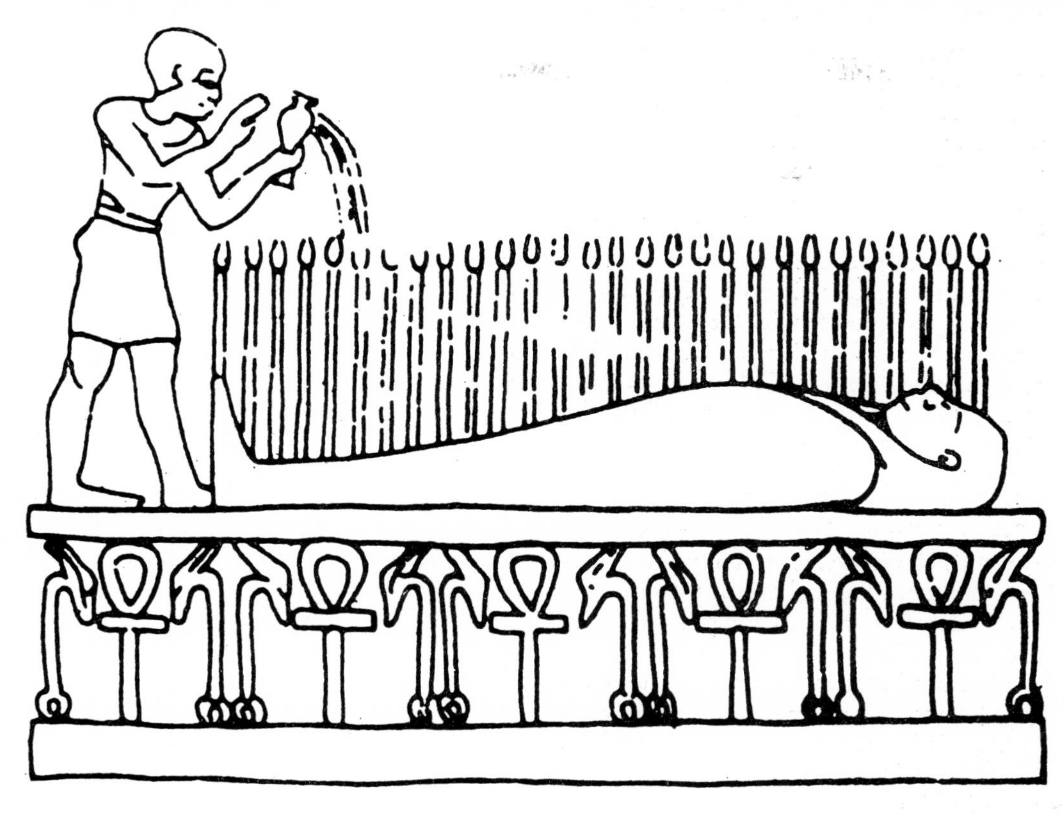

33

the ritual gesture of worship: Isis, Nephthys, Horus and Amun.
No image represents the significance of the myth better. If we doubted it, another bas-relief at Philae would emphasise it again. On it we see the body of the god in his narrow mummy case, stretched out on the ground, in profile. This time the stalks rise from the actual body, as if from humus. The representation of *Osiris vegetating* corresponds to certain customs of the ancient Egyptians. They modelled small clay figurines of the deity and planted seeds in them, which soon grew green and covered the simulacrum. In other words the renaissance of Osiris and that of the vegetation were looked on as concomitant facts. The criminal act of Seth who threw his brother's body into the Nile was betrayed by the flooding of the waters, because the dead man revived immediately to liberate the stream of life. A later tradition identifies the flood with 'the sweat' of Osiris.
The hymns to Osiris sometimes have a special ardour and lyricism. They express affection or joy, depending on the episodes of the legend, with an almost romantic energy. Should this surprise us? He is the one who is awaited, the one from whom life is expected, the divine water bearer.

33

32

Seth, his adversary, is an antithetical figure. In contrast he represents dryness and aridity. We understand the bitterness of the struggle between the two enemies, although they had the same father: Geb, the earth, and the same mother: Nut, the sky. This struggle clearly recalls the struggle which took place in Egypt every year and which is still taking place. Drying out and inundation are opposed there; there is no gradual change from one to the other with the intermediate seasons we have in Europe. The burning wind has the violence of Seth.

Is not Osiris the closest to us of all the Egyptian gods? He constantly appeals to the emotions. He is betrayed, martyred; he calls for justice. Far from being the guarantor of the privileges of a minority, we see him grant his blessings to everybody: he democratises eternal life and that is why his cult continually increased in popularity during the last millennium B.C. With him, we are not confronted with a theological concept. The other Egyptian gods are transcendent. He is immanent. He lives his 'passion'. The men of the end of Antiquity already sense in him what they are looking for: a god who assumes their condition and who, by having assumed it, saves them by his own humanity – and by hope.

Isis and Osiris are in perfect harmony. Admittedly Isis is a formidable magician. With the mud which she moistens with her saliva we surprise her making a serpent, then she animates the reptile and orders it to go and bite Re, the sun god, whose inheritance she covets. The god begs Isis to cure him. She demands that he tells her his true name. Re has to agree to this. Once mistress of the divine name, the magician is omnipotent: she casts a spell on her victim. His power also serves her for better purposes; she uses it against Seth, to help Horus and Osiris.

All the same that is only one aspect of a complex figure. Isis knows how to play the role of the faithful wife, she who wishes to bury her beloved piously, who even tries to revive him with her own breath. She is also the anxious mother, she hides her child, brings him up far from danger, supports him in battle.

The empire of Isis is immense. A hymn confirms it: 'I am the mother of all nature, mistress of all the elements, origin and principal of the centuries, supreme divinity, queen of the spirits, first among the inhabitants of the sky, unique among gods and goddesses. The luminous summits of the sky, the salutary breezes of the sea, the desolate silences of hell, it is I who govern all at my will.' (Quoted by Serge Sauneron, in the *Dictionnaire de la Civilisation égyptienne.)* We should remember these words when we see the proud silhouette engraved on the pylons of Philae.

Powerful and maternal. How could the men of Egypt who had seen their gods abandon them to the invaders and prove quite inadequate to protect them, how could they help but turn, as a last resort, to a divinity who was both tender and magical? Isis was 'the lady of Philae': first she took precedence over Hathor and later over her divine husband. Until the fifth century A.D. pilgrims came to worship her, heaping her with offerings, when the other gods of antiquity were erased from men's memories: one of the last texts in her honour dates to + 473. Owing to her, Philae was one of the last citadels of paganism. But what still led believers to Isis merged with what destroyed the ancient cults: she was asked to be the helping one, the merciful, she who intercedes – and men had already discovered another image of intercession long before.

3

4

May Isis and Osiris preside over every visit to Philae! And may the magician fan the

34

35 ►

prostrate body in the temples with her wings to restore the living breath to him! The stones need this intimate association with a great dream.

'Everything here is recent,' cried Champollion in 1829, in a hurry to press on. We shall not be so scornful. Even if the builders were content to re-employ the directives of the Early Period in the greater part of the work, at least it is not a slavish unthinking copy, and the notion of facsimile is relative when religion is in command. The temple of Isis at Philae is not the equivalent of the Parisian church of Sainte-Clotilde! We are not such purists that the adulterations by foreign grafts repel us. They are not always without charm. And they always witness to the heavy passage of history and the destiny of peoples.

Towards −452, Herodotus visited the island of Elephantine, opposite present-day Aswan, and went no further. Was the historian wrongly informed or was Philae really negligible? In fact the cult of Isis there must have gone back to remote epochs, as the re-employment of certain materials in the more recent constructions shows, in particular a stone used in the columns of the pronaos bearing a cartouche of the Pharaoh Amasis (26th dynasty, 568–526 B.C.).

There is a sort of 'prehistory' of Philae. Only the later pages of its history are known to us. This history begins in the fourth century B.C., which is absurdly modern for Egypt. One of the sovereigns of the 30th dynasty (from −378 to −341) began the work on the great temple of Isis. They were the last 'indigenous' Pharaohs. Which of them really undertook the work, Nectanebo I (−378–360) or Nectanebo II (−359–341)? During the reign of the former, Artaxerxes II Mnemon ordered the satrap Pharnabazus to reconquer Egypt. The Persian army was at the gates of Memphis, but the satrap did not take advantage of his rapid advance; he waited and his expedition ended in a rout (−373). The Persian threat was put off for a

◄ 36

time – Artaxerxes III Ochus did not retake Egypt until −345 – and this respite undoubtedly enabled Nectanebo I to undertake various buildings, those at Philae among others. Nevertheless it was during the Greek epoch (−330–30), under the domination of the Ptolemies, that the isle was given monuments to match the growing importance of the cult which was celebrated there. The Romans finished these works left uncompleted by their predecessors and they executed new ones: it was in the first and second centuries A.D. that Philae experienced its apogee. Its principal monuments extend over at least six centuries.

The buildings occupy the southern part of the island, undoubtedly because they began from a primitive chapel situated there which the constructors were bent on turning into a large sanctuary. Incidentally, you should make your way into the island by the south shore – or, if you prefer, by the little porch called the 'pavilion' of Nectanebo. The columns of this edifice flare out into capitals shaped like open calyxes, but they are only a first 'storey', for the corolla supports a cube representing on its four faces the triangular face of a woman with cow's ears, the goddess Hathor. There follows an abacus, whose rectangular sides are decorated with the representation of a naos. This last 'storey' succeeds directly to the former one: we may see in it not only the secret part of the sanctuary, but also the very place where the sistrum sounded, the favourite instrument of a deity who presided over dancing and music – and whose own face recalls the shape of the instrument.

22

So Hathor welcomes the visitor. She will accompany him. It is impossible to forget that she is one of the major divinities: cow goddess, she is 'the mother of the divine falcon or the sun'. At Thebes, at Memphis, she was sovereign of the Mountain of the Dead, while still remaining regent of the sky. Sometimes depicted in the actual form of the animal – as in the relief and the painted sandstone at Deir el-Bahri – she may show herself in the guise of a young woman whose head is decorated with horns enclosing the solar disc.

She is present in the proliferating force of the trees and also manifests herself as the magical 'Lady of the Sycamore Tree'. Fierce, she transforms herself into a lioness if need be to punish the impious, but her cult was mainly celebrated under the sign of gaiety.

Hathor's functions are numerous. Some of them overlap with those of Isis. She suckles the child Horus, whose mother – and wife – she also is. So we may think that at first she shared Philae with Isis, but that the latter finally prevailed over her rival and increasingly monopolised the fervour of the faithful at the courts of the Late Period. However that may be, Ptolemy VI Philometor (–180 –145) had a small temple built for Hathor, 23 to the east, quite near the second pylon. Its building and decoration were continued by Ptolemy VIII Euergetes II (–170–164) and the Roman Augustus. In it we can see the latter offering a sacrifice to . . . to Hathor! A strange image to adjoin a cartouche in the name of Cleopatra, last of the Ptolemies. The edifice, modest though it may be, nevertheless shows the persistent presence of Hathor on the island of Isis.

The avenue *(dromos)* which leads to the great temple is lined by two porticoes. The one to the east is unfinished. To the west the columns of the colonnade – called after Augustus and Tiberius – have capitals which more than once exhibit fresh floral invention. But we must admit that the perspective of 34 the dromos is not very satisfactory, as the western portico is much more oblique than the eastern one. Moreover they conceal some of the façade so that only about two-thirds of it is revealed. So the great façade of the temple is partly spoilt. Nor is it helped by the absence of two obelisks which were taken to England.

But let us admit that this façade is still fine enough to delight a traveller approaching it with an open mind. There is no doubt about its generosity and majesty. 34 And the decoration of this pylon, though 'decadent', still retains energy and nobility. On the façade of the western tower we find the repetition of a scene which was always 'topical' from the palette of King Narmer onwards (i.e. since the Thinite epoch, –3000 –2650). Once 19 again, Pharaoh brandishes his weapon in his right hand and in the left he seizes by the hair a handful of enemies who implore his mercy. The movement is stiff, borrowed, devoid of that assurance, that masterful vitality we find at Abu Simbel in the effigy of the glorious Ramesses II in a similar situation. In fact the sovereign here is Ptolemy Neos Dionysos, whose difficult reign already announced the end of a dynasty. This massacre of prisoners is offered to Isis, whose relief was carved at the Christian epoch. The warlike scene is surmounted by two scenes showing offerings, peaceful like those which decorate the upper part of the eastern tower.

At the foot of the latter, to the right of the entrance portal, are the tall processionary images of Isis (leading) and Hathor, and between them falcon-headed Horus, protector of the king and king himself. 18 Two grooves are cut out on either side of the entrance portal. In them we should imagine the flagpoles on which standards were hoisted to stream in the wind above the temple. In the left-hand tower, to the west, a door opens onto two halls which lead to the *mammisi*. The word (borrowed by Champollion from the Coptic religion) designates 'the place of birth'. It is a place of mystery: every year Isis brought her son, the god Horus, into the world there. In the temples of the Late Period – at Dendera, Edfu and Philae – this edifice appears as an annex where the goddess made a retreat to give birth to the third personage of the Osirian triad. When you enter the courtyard of the temple at Philae, you immediately find, on the left, between the reverse of the first pylon and the second pylon, the portico of the *mammisi*, 37 ►

16, 17

which has done so much for the island's celebrity. The 'Hathoric' columns, separated by intercolumnar walls, are like those which we have already seen in the pavilion of Nectanebo: they terminate in the effigy of Hathor on the faces of a cube, surmounted by the image of a naos. But the capitals are complicated: the very varied floral motives are treated in vigorous masses, the different elements intertwining powerfully rather than sensitively. The decoration, mainly the work of Ptolemy Euergetes, recalls the birth and childhood of Horus. This portico corresponds, not quite symmetrically, to the one which lines the eastern side of the courtyard and gives access to the rooms of a sort of sacristy.

38

The dimensions of the second pylon, the northern boundary of the courtyard, are smaller than the first one and it is clearly not parallel to it, but slanting from south-east to north-east. Once again Ptolemy Neos Dionysos sacrifices to the gods on it. At the foot of the right-hand tower, in the centre, there is a strange projection. It is a rough embedded granite block. However its face has been cut and polished so that an inscription commemorating a donation by Ptolemy Philometor could be engraved on it. The central gate of the pylon leads into a hypostyle hall, from which the naos is entered.
Here it is a good idea to stop and turn round. To the south the gates succeed each other and open onto the Nile in the distance. So the effigy of the goddess looks towards the river which, like a source of life, comes towards her from the horizon.
The Holy Boat, on which Isis went to Bigah every ten days for the libations in honour of her husband Osiris, left from the naos. Every year she paid a visit to her worshippers on the neighbouring banks. The carrying of the boat to the water is recalled by the bas-reliefs which decorate the reverse of the first pylon to the west, some of them admirably drawn. The famous 'kiosk of Trajan', so popularised by tourist posters, was one of the stations on this sacred journey.

21
38

35 32

5

Such was the group of buildings threatened by the construction of the Sadd El Aali, the new dam, upstream from the first one.
Far from destroying the monuments, as might have been feared, the latter had, if anything, preserved them, and this was a pleasant surprise. For nine months of the year the island was swallowed up, but it reappeared faithfully, it lived. Out of fear that the current might sap the base of the temples, their foundations were consolidated, a wise precautionary measure which certainly prevented subsidences.
The new project was a far more serious threat. It envisaged the establishment of a reach between the two dams. Then Philae would be in the sheet of water between the old construction downstream and the new one upstream. Admittedly the level in this reservoir would be lower than the level to be attained behind the new dam and actually lower than the present maximum height. There would be a sort of landing. The mass of water enclosed would only reach about halfway up the principal pylon of the temple of Isis.

39

Was this an advance? By no means. Never again would the island be completely exposed for part of the year. It would no longer have a 'dry season'! On the other hand – and here lay the deadly peril – the mass of water would be subject to daily variations in height of more than eighteen feet. The resulting up and down movement would ultimately 'file away' the walls. To use a simile, the buildings would undergo a suction comparable to that of a lollipop going in and out of a child's mouth. They would grow thinner and thinner until they collapsed.

In 1955 Mr. Osman Rostem denounced the anticipated catastrophe in a definitive study, *The salvage of Philae*. And he proposed a remedy: '... the isolation of the island from the rest of the reservoir by a series of small dams around it, dams which would protect the temples from submersion, at the same time saving them from the disturbances involved if there was an excessive increase in the level, or if they were transferred.'

These last words alluded to projects already established (and abandoned) in 1902, which had been modified but taken up again in their essential details. The idea had been to dismantle and reconstruct the monuments of Philae on a new foundation. Some people proposed transporting and rebuilding them on the neighbouring island of Bigah.

These undertakings would have taken a long time, more time than was available, and would have cost too much. In addition it was unlikely that the time-worn temples and porticoes could have stood up to such handling.

M. Rostem's idea was justified by the topography. It was enough to look at a map. A dam between the north bank and the island of Agilkieh, a second dam between that island and Bigah, and a third between Bigah and the east bank would form a semi-circular rampart connecting the protective masses of the islands. Philae is fortunate enough to be situated on the interior of a sort of arc, the natural segments of which can be united.

39

Such is the project which was adopted. The government of the Netherlands proposed to pursue the study free of charge. It was entrusted to the Dutch engineers of Nedeco who worked in agreement whith the Egyptian specialised services.

How would Philae look once the dam was built? It was decided that the level of the water in the shelter of this vast rampart would be so maintained that the whole of the island would be permanently above the surface as it had been for centuries. The comparison with a double boiler has been much used to describe it. We shall have to use it again, for lack of a better one: Philae was to be inside a receptacle which would itself swim in a larger receptacle containing the water of the reach. To tell the truth the comparison is not quite accurate, for it does not take into account the bank and its natural surroundings. It would be wrong to imagine the island at the bottom of a vast bowl.

As you can imagine, what seems easy to plan is very difficult to put into practice. It is not the purpose of this book to describe the difficulties or the solutions put forward. That field belongs to the experts and technicians. The problem of watertightness, for example, called for countless studies before the decision was made to build a pumping station which would get rid of the water constantly infiltrating the basin of Philae. The cost of the whole enterprise was estimated at 6 million dollars. In a message to Congress in April 1960 President Kennedy announced the allocation of that sum for the protection of the island.

Philae was saved. The works will begin in 1968.

The hour has come to listen joyfully to the musicians whose image decorates the stone of the *mammisi* and the temple of Hathor. May the god Bes play the flute, the harp and the tambourine!

Towards the year 360 A.D. the island's last sacred falcon, the symbol of Horus, was killed. In 550 Justinian closed the temple of Isis, but the bishop of Aswan reopened it seven years later, transforming the pronaos into a church. Egypt had become Christian. A modest basilica stood on the northern section, between a temple of Horus the Avenger, a chapel dedicated to Augustus and a Roman arch. Large effigies were carved. Byzantine crosses were engraved on the

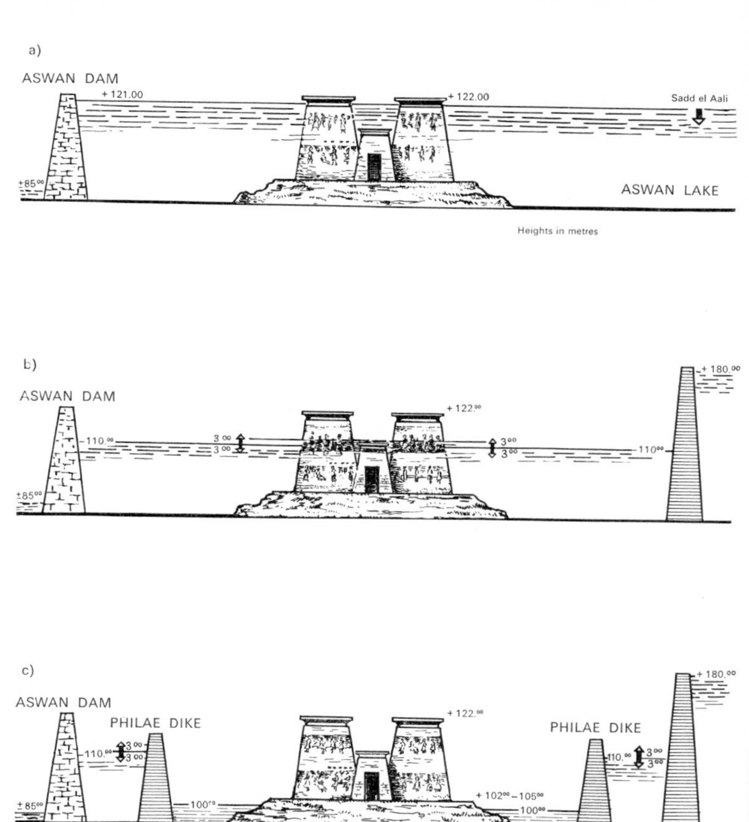

39 *Diagram of Philae.* The engraving on the left shows: *a)* The fate of Philae since the construction of the first Aswan dam. Using the great temple of Isis, the highest monument on the island, as a scale, we see that the river only allows the tops of the pylon to emerge at high water. *b)* If the temple had been left in the basin contained between the old and the new dam about a third of the façade would have been permanently above water, but variations in the water level would have eaten away the monument in the end. *c)* The solution adopted: Philae is surrounded by protective dykes which isolate it inside the storage lake. It becomes an island again. The temples are permanently exposed. Right: map of the valley between the old and the new dam. The situation of Philae, towards the top, between other islands, means that protective dykes can be built. These dykes abut onto the islands, inter-connect them and shelter Philae behind a semi-circular wall (represented by dark lines on the map).
Taken from 'Comment Philae sera sauvée' by Michel Conil Lacoste (*Courrier de l'Unesco,* October 1961).

walls, among the reliefs where Pharaoh still went on sacrificing to Isis, sister-bride of Osiris, and Hathor, deity of love.
I have never felt that these crosses, very close to the Egyptian *ankh* which is the sign of life, are an outrage to the ancient Philae. From here, from this islet among the sands and the rocks, the cult of Isis was to reach the Roman world and offer it a mystery contrary to Latin reason.
Certain places are made so that the gods may succeed each other in them and witness to the same desire, the same hope and the same will in men to free the mind from terror and death. The basic images of the same dream were engraved here at Philae for centuries.

Prelude to Kalabsha

◄ 41

The island of Elephantine, opposite Aswan, has had a peculiar workshop on it for a long time.
Chipped stones on the ground, which might be fragments of a broken pavement.... Elsewhere fragments of cornices, architraves and lintels supported by props. Farther on, large packing cases with the shaft of some column or the floral detail of a capital visible between their slats; others completely closed, containing perhaps a bas-relief or a sculpture. There are figures and letters on the blocks and cases – all the marks of an inventory.
Three monuments lie there, awaiting resurrection: the temple of Debod, the kiosk of Kertassi and the chapel of Tafa.

They were the first to be rescued. From the summer of 1960 onwards full details of their component parts, their situation, their construction and inscriptions had been taken down, a task carried out with remarkable speed solely during the low water period. Teams immediately dismantled them, then transported the indexed pieces on the large Nile barges known as *sandals*. One after the other the three buildings – first Debod, then Kertassi and lastly Tafa – sailed to the island of Elephantine where they looked like a great archaeological junk yard. All these monuments had been neighbours. Debod was 10, Kertassi 28 and Tafa 33 miles from Aswan.

For them, it was only a stage on their journey. The temple of Debod and the chapel of Kertassi are to be offered in thanks by the United Arab Republic to two of the foreign countries which have contributed to the rescue campaign. Let us give our imagination full rein! Tomorrow, perhaps, the porticoes of Debod will rise in some American museum, like those New York 'cloisters' where Romanesque and Gothic remains have been reassembled and rebuilt – quite

◄ 42

successfully. But the kiosk of Kertassi will not emigrate. It will be reconstructed on a cliff in Nubia.

The adventure is a lucky one for these monuments. Less consolidated than Philae, they have suffered from the long annual submersion. The columns of Kertassi had collapsed in spite of the 1908 restoration; one of them rested on an intercolumnar wall. A quadrilateral entirely filled with a chaos of disjointed blocks: that was what the chapel of Tafa looked like. As for the temple of Debod, it had suffered severe damage during the 1868 earthquake.
During the summer season there were few tourists who stopped at the ruins, which were then high and dry, but disappointing. They were for the archaeologists. Later, when they are reconstructed, it will be possible to see the buildings more easily – and at least as they appeared to travellers in the nineteenth century.

They are 'recent' monuments. Debod, the most important, was probably built by the Ethiopian king Arq-Amon, in the time of Ptolemy IV Philopator, about –210. Ptolemy Euergetes II had decorated it with an imposing pink granite naos. The emperors Augustus and Tiberius were found on the façade among the Egyptian gods.

With its two Hathoric entrance pillars and its four columns with floral capitals, the kiosk of Kertassi must have resembled the kiosk of Trajan at Philae, which was certainly its contemporary. Tafa displays a Ptolemaic and Roman style. In other words, nothing was very ancient.

41

What was the artistic worth of these monuments? Tafa profited a good deal from its situation at the entrance to a wild granite gorge which we shall mention again later, upstream from Kalabsha. But the kiosk of Kertassi, built on a sandstone promontory, enchanted nineteenth-century travellers.
'A small solitary bouquet of graceful columns...' That was how Amelia B. Edwards saw it in 1874. And the astonishing traveller (to whom British archaeology owes such a debt) adds that she was reminded of the temple of Poseidon on Cape Sunium. Perhaps that is going too far. But even in 1850 Maxime du Camp, one of Flaubert's three companions in Egypt, expressed his frank enthusiasm (in *Le Nil, Egypte et Nubie*): '... The elegant ruins of a small sanctuary of Hathor stand on a conical hill which dominates the Nile and the desert. One is surprised to find a slender delicate temple in these countries full of Cyclopean buildings. It is the work of time which has made it so charming; it has knocked down the walls and the terrace, and left nothing standing but two columns and two pillars silhouetted against the blue sky. The columns, connected by a monolithic architrave some sixteen feet long, have lotus capitals. The square pillars, still encumbered with the jambs of a broken gate, are surmounted by a head of Hathor, surrounded by fillets and crowned with a small temple, her special headdress; no inscription gives the date of construction which appears to go back to the Roman emperors. Through the spaces between the columns you see the horizon of verdant palm trees and the meanders of the river.'

42

These edifices (and some others) were situated, let us recall, in the region of Lower Nubia which formed the Dodekaschoinos of the Ptolemies and the *collimitium* of the Romans, between Philae and Takompso. The Romans looked on it as a distant boundary of the Empire and still more as a troubled zone where order was constantly threatened.

Troops were quartered at several points. The remains of a military establishment have been discovered at Tafa – the ancient Taphis. But Kertassi is the place where you can still see what the Roman occupation was and understand its difficulties. A pink sandstone quarry in which a small sanctuary in the form of a speos is hollowed out still exists south of the kiosk. It is entered by a handsome door surmounted by a winged disc and friezes of *uraei*. On either side, two busts in Roman style have been sculptured out of the solid rock in high relief, although not very successfully. Other figures, crude and sometimes only rough-hewn, seem to spring from the wall: mother goddesses, ill-defined personages, lions' heads, gargoyles. The names of emperors are also legible: Antoninus Pius, Marcus Aurelius, Severus, Caracalla. This rocky front bears handsome inscriptions in Greek characters: the Roman officers had them carved in commemoration of their stay in this remote garrison.

Some distance away there is an enclosure fortified with bastions. So Kertassi presented the appearance of an armed outpost. In the second and third centuries the quarry supplied the stone necessary for the monuments of the region. The stone which was used for the buildings at Philae came from it. So it was essential to protect Kertassi from any form of attack.

Kalabsha

45

46

Towards Tafa the river's mood changes. Its surface is shot through with quivers and vibrations. Soon the boat avoids eddies, moves away from the tangled clumps of driftwood and goes round whirlpools. A great shaft of water shudders under the hull. On the banks the scenery too changes. The long border of sandstone which we followed from Philae seems to move away westwards. What approaches is dark, almost black. Granite scree descends into the Nile, sometimes giving way to abrupt cliffs. The valley becomes choked up. The horizon seems to close. We cross Bab Kalabsha, the 'gate of handcuffs', the ledge of hard rock which the river has forced, the barrier through which it has had to struggle to clear a passage. For some five miles the water is turbulent, rebellious, angry.

On the other side, once through the narrows, we find the vast calm stream again. If you go up the river the mouth of a wadi soon opens on the right, completely blocked by sand from the Libyan desert. Once again the villages begin to crown the ridges. One of them on the west bank is strung out like a festoon of white cubes across the rocky slope, above a sort of blockhouse whose grey walls are on the cracked bed of the mud, very close to the water in summer.

The village is Kalabsha. The heavy mass like a concrete fort is the temple. *43*

2

At first sight, there is nothing exalting and we are prepared to be disappointed.

In this the most important Nubian monument, after Philae and Abu Simbel? Undoubtedly it is in its dimensions, but not when it comes to elegance or proportions. Its heaviness betrays the absence of real strength. This indeed is a Roman work. Massive, powerful, but genius has deserted it. The pylon, not parallel to the rest of the buildings, has lost its upper part, which has collapsed. It seems to sprawl rather than stand up and impress. There is no decoration on its two towers, no great representations which would transform them into living screens. The entrance portico alone displays some ornamentation: beneath a gorge destroyed in the centre there is a beautiful winged disc flanked by two *uraei* puffing themselves up, and on the lintel there are the remains of reliefs, on the left, in particular, a rather conventional offering scene. The rest is bare yellowish-grey stone, marked near its present-day summits by a light-coloured band which indicates the level of the annual submersion.

At ground level, on the right, a wall prolongs the façade. It is pierced by a door which gave onto a guard-house. A similar wall rose on the left; it is almost destroyed. These are the components of an enclosure. When you land and look at the front of the edifice you are really confronted by a fortress with no detail to give the lie to the first general impression.

Now let us walk round the monument. Let us walk along one of its sides and climb the flinty cliff which backs it. Soon we have a bird's eye view of its different parts. Its internal anatomy is revealed to us. A model unfolds before our eyes, seen from the rear, in isometric projection.

44

This is where all the schoolboys in the world should be brought (or should have been brought, for the edifice is to be transferred) to illustrate lessons about ancient Egypt!

They would have a clear view of the primary structure of a temple. They would 'spell out' the syllables which compose it, starting from the farthest end. First of all, some sixty feet from the river, the pylon facing east. It opens onto a courtyard, lined on three sides by a peristyle.

Next a powerful main building whose summit forms a rectangle on which columns used to support a roof now vanished; it is the hypostyle hall of the pronaos. Lower than the pylon, it still dominates the next building. The latter contains three halls which are sanctuaries, and in the last of them was the naos, the 'house of God' in which the effigy of the divinity stood. Let us add that this hall ingeniously concealed in its walls a secret staircase which led to a hiding place for treasure – and that the king alone had the right to enter the naos, a right which he transferred to the high priest, the representative responsible for officiating in his name. The plan of Kalabsha is simple compared with that of other temples. There is no need to explain it further. Let us confine ourselves to giving our schoolchildren a summary plan from the top of our cliff, the light and shade picking at the shapes for us.

A few more details. A tall wall, supported to the east on the extremities of the pylon, surrounds the temple on three sides: thus it demarcates a sort of ambulatory around the main halls which we shall have occasion to walk round later.

The construction as a whole is further protected by a surrounding wall, and it is inside this that the priests' living quarters were probably situated; also inside, but to the south, to the right of a lateral door, is a small building which may be the ruins of a *mammisi,* the mysterious place where the goddess gave birth to the child king.

Such, viewed from above, is the great temple whose well considered design shows up clearly against the river and the dry horizon. This simple structure contrasts with a fugitive contourless landscape. It asserts itself in a kind of void. The sky is too vast here, the space too open and gaping for us to remain insensitive to this self-contained, organised, composed mass. In this series of volumes a statement is hammered out. There is no denying that it is the argument

of authority, for what use would nuances be against the absolute of the dried up distances, on the edge of a river between two deserts? This brings us to a confession. We are afraid of having exaggerated our first judgment. Suddenly Kalabsha assumes its meaning from this inchoate absurd environment. It even finds its grandeur in it.
Austere, abstract, no doubt. But now it is time to climb down the cliff again and enter the temple.

3

Everything changes. Once past the pylon the bareness of the exterior is broken. We take off the shell.
Of course it is a question of contrast. The temple is less decorated than most. In the hypostyle hall only the wall of the west door has reliefs. Those in the first hall are unfinished (paintings decorated them, it is true, but they have been effaced by the submersions since 1902). But the walls of the second and third halls are covered with representations. Some large figures are inscribed on the stones of the ambulatory, which are sometimes ineptly divided into panels; we shall come across them later. It is not a complex with lavish decoration in comparison with other buildings of the Late Period, those of Kom Ombo or Edfu, for example.
Nevertheless from the entrance, in the courtyard, you experience a feeling of growth and blossoming induced by the sight of the columns of the peristyle and the hypostyle. They are crowned with expansive floral capitals, and connected, just in front of the hypostyle hall, by low walls on which the king and the gods are shown. A broken statue of Tuthmosis III (–1504 –1450) found near the pylon and a bas-relief in the sanctuary representing Amenhotep II (–1450–1425) permit us to attribute the foundation of the first temple to these two sovereigns. We are, of course, confronted with a reconstruction from the Graeco-Roman period. In the third hall, a relief shows the emperor Augustus sacrificing.

47

These late additions give the decoration a 'style' which many judge harshly, if they do not actually banish it to the museum of decadent errors! People are fond of talking of the bastardised academicism of the reliefs, of their borrowed or stilted character, their rigidity – or their affectation. Some scholars denounce the puffy faces, a general flabbiness, the clumsy figures.
Let us see what pleasure we can get out of this decoration without lowering our aesthetic standards. Mannerism is not always to be proscribed. At Kalabsha it contributes a certain charm to images which linger in the mind's eye.
To begin with, those of Mandulis. A local god, patron of the temple, he seems to be a Nubian avatar of Horus. It would have been better to write 'the Mandulises'! For he appears in a 'young' and an 'old' aspect. Young, he wears a curly tress of hair on his right temple, which habitually indicates childhood – and perhaps he is going to suck the thumb he holds to his mouth? Old, he wears the heaviest of the pharaonic head-dresses, the insignia of power and glory.

49

In the ambulatory the west internal wall has been polished so that a large 'picture' (5 feet 11 inches wide; 6 feet 2 inches high) could be engraved on it. It depicts the two Mandulises face to face. The Egyptologist H. Gauthier, in his monograph on the temple of Kalabsha, sees the *king* Mandulis on the right and the god Mandulis on the left. The former is clothed in a rich complicated costume. One of his hands holds the sceptre, the other the ansate cross, the *ankh,* the sign of life. Two more *ankhs* are stuck into an unusual coiffure. In front of this symbol a vigorous falcon, topped with the solar disc, spreads his wings, as if to welcome the emblem, protect it and open the way to it. The attitude of the god on the left repeats

51

that of the king. He holds the same attributes, *ankh* and sceptre, in his hands. But the costume is quite different: a head of Horus decorates the pectoral; the loin-cloth is composed of crossed feathers, like a pleated skirt! As for the crown, it piles up on the horizontal horns of the ram, attribute of the god Khnum, *uraei,* ostrich feathers, discs, floral elements, etc. – a heavy set piece, an edifice of symbols of power. On either side of the divine face is a small *uraeus,* the image of the burning eye of Re, the flame which protects.

On a bell-shaped altar between the two effigies is the offering of bread and flowers. The 'picture' is surmounted by a sunken pediment. Holes have been pierced in the wall at regular intervals round the relief. Undoubtedly a naos (or a tabernacle) was once embedded in the stone, held in place by tenons fixed in the holes.

The significance of the image and of its late style are debatable. However the dual and unique Mandulis was especially worshipped here. And the relief, now in the full light of day, has grandeur, rhythm and energy in our opinion.

The same qualities are found – though still more pronounced – in the pictures which are inscribed on the outside wall of the sanctuary, in the ambulatory, on the upper register. Two 'family' triads are going to meet a Mandulis. Each triad is walking in a different direction from the other, the two Mandulises remaining at the two extremities. Thus the decoration comprises two groups of four figures back to back.

On the right the king holds out a censer and makes a libation on an altar piled with flowers and bread. In front of him Osiris, Isis and Horus succeed each other, walking from left to right. The relief of the picture was not finished and it is badly damaged. We must say a little more about the other group. In it the movement is the opposite: the gods walk from right to left, towards the king on the extreme left, almost bordering the wall. Soberly dressed, wearing a simple crown, he is offering incense. He offers it first to Isis, the nearest to him, then to Horus, bearer of the *shent,* and lastly to the *god* Mandulis, recognisable by the emblematic tiara which generally surmounts his representations in the temple. These are large figures: that of the king is 11 feet 6 inches high. The picture is 23 feet 2 inches wide. The work exhibits undoubted care in its execution. Of all the reliefs at Kalabsha it is the most accomplished.

Other images have been carved beneath this noble and serene frieze. It does not look as if there was much thought given to their arrangement. They give the impression of something added, even superadded. Their scriptorial quality is weak. Some of them will hold the visitor's attention by their strangeness. Thus a *uraeus* which terminates in a human head wearing horns, the ordinary attribute of the goddess, undulates and rears beneath the upright feet of Isis. A few inches away, Isis holds out the sign of life to a bird-soul bearing the crown of Mandulis. Further on, on the other side of a scene of offering drawn with more assurance, we find two *human-headed* birds exactly alike. The right-hand one is perched on a *uraeus* incorporating the solar disc. They appear to look at each other in the course of a sort of conversation. In fact this arrangement inevitably recalls that of the two Mandulises in the large picture we have already mentioned.

50

Was the bird-soul a form of the local god? That is what H. Gauthier suggested. In any case the representation is repeated like a graphic leit motiv on the walls of the temple. M[me] Desroches-Noblecourt has remarked on its frequence. The outside north wall of the pronaos has a scene which has become famous. Perched on the *uraeus,* the bird is once again crowned with the diadem of Mandulis. It stands out against a bush of lotus stalks. The buds, the blossoming

55

49

50

53

flowers open above the human head in a radiating arc of life.
So Kalabsha gives a fine picture of one of the three spiritual principles on which Egypt based eternal life: the *ba,* the divine power to manifest itself in the most various forms. The temple was transformed into a church in the sixth century. Curiously, the bird-ba of the pronaos has remained intact, whereas the effigies of Isis and the king which surround it have been savagely knocked about.
Undoubtedly the Christians recognised an image of the soul – and respected it.

4

Kalabsha is established on the site of the ancient Talmis which was the capital of the Dodekaschoinos. Undoubtedly the looting Blemmyes frequented the temple during the decline of the Roman domination. They came to worship Mandulis and Wadjet there, indigenous avatars of Horus and Isis. They settled in the region and dominated it. The threat they represented is attested by an inscription on one of the low intercolumnar walls of the pronaos. On it King Silko sings his own praises and triumphs. This proclamation is naively emphatic but it deserves partial quotation, because it throws light on the history of Nubia about 550 A.D. 'I, Silko, king of the Nobatae and all the Ethiopians, I came twice to Talmis (Kalabsha) and Taphis (Tafa). I fought the Blemmyes and God gave me the victory three against one. I conquered them again and took their towns and established myself there with my hordes. The first time I conquered and they implored me for mercy; I made peace with them and they swore allegiance to me on their idols, and I trusted their oath because they are people of honour (...) I am a lion in the lower country and a bear in the upper country. I fought the Blemmyes of Talmis at Primis (Ibrim) once again, and the other Nobatae of the upper regions; I ravaged their territory because they had sought a quarrel with me. The princes of other peoples who attack me, I do not let them sit in the shade unless they beg my permission; they may not drink wine in their houses, for I carry off the wives and children of those who attack me...'
As we see, our Christian king did not have an easy time of it! A very long time afterwards, in the nineteenth century, travellers used to complain about the people of Kalabsha. From what they say this aggressive people, hating foreigners, strongly disliked anyone taking an interest in 'its' temple, however staunch a Moslem he might be! Arms in hand, they threatened visitors, forced them to beat a retreat and regain their boat as fast as possible – or, when in their best mood, forced them to pay an excessive 'entrance fee'.

The historian and archaeologist Louis-A. Christophe has published the picturesque and adventurous accounts of ill-treated travellers and archaeologists (*La Revue du Caire,* April 1961). This is the answer given to Thomas Legh's guide in 1813: 'How do these people dare to come here? Do they not know that we have five hundred guns in our village and that Daoud Kachef himself had not the courage to come and raise taxes from us?' An identical misadventure befell Jean-Baptiste Belzoni in 1816: 'When we entered the temple immediately after landing, there was no one at the door. But when we wanted to leave, we found a great number of people assembled at the entrance of the pylon. We prepared to pass through the door, but they completely blocked it, demanding money from us. They were all armed with lances, shields, halberds, etc.'
Here, our scholarly Italian traveller is going to vie with the heroic king Silko! He goes on in these terms: 'I told them that I did not

◄ 54

want to obtain our freedom to pass with money, but that if they let us leave, I would do what I felt suitable. And I left them no time for reflection; I walked straight ahead looking them full in the face and no one touched us... When we had passed through, I gave them a tip and I added that I was prepared to pay them a larger sum if they brought me some antiquities. They understood me and thus I bought several sepulchral stones bearing Greek inscriptions.'

Haven't the inhabitants of Kalabsha been over-maligned? Travel in Nubia was arduous, it resembled an expedition, the difficulties had to be dwelt on... It is not our intention to impugn the narrators' good faith. But we have other accounts in which similar 'perils' are not recalled. By no means all visitors were helped on with the toe of a boot. Nothing so romantic is to be found in other authors. Let us see what they had to say. James Mangles (in 1823), Champollion, Jean-Jacques Ampère and Flaubert, to mention a few, are not so moving. We would be better advised to think that the natives had changing moods and widely varying degrees of welcome – depending on the absence or presence of the janissaries! The Barabra, the Qenus (such are the names of the peoples of the region, westernised as Barbarins) had grouped their houses of dried mud around the temple at the beginning of the nineteenth century. Sometimes, said a traveller, they clung on to it like wasps' nests. The interior courtyard even served as a caravanserai and nomads camped in the pronaos. In fact this proximity of animals and human beings was an ancient custom. A decree engraved not far from the proclamation of Silko (dating from about 250 A.D.) gives the order to chase the pigs out of the town. So we can imagine boars, sows and porkers grunting among the august ruins. In any case the columns were used for bill-sticking.

This promiscuity was put to rights, mainly by the construction of the first dam. The houses were forced to shift to the heights of the cliff out of the way of the annual flood. But a chaos of stone still covered the soil of the interior courtyard, undoubtedly as the result of an earthquake. In 1907–1908 the engineer Barsanti remedied these subsidences and dislocations.

At the time of our first visit to Kalabsha in February 1960, at the time of high water, all we saw of the temple was what emerges for nine months of the year: two small moles and a rectangular quay in the stream, the tops of the pylon and the upper part of the pronaos, a little more than at Philae. During our stay in 1961, at the end of summer, the spectacle was quite different. The German Federal Republic had decided to save the building from the total immersion to come. Large boats which acted as hotels and laboratories for the engineers were moored to the muddy bank. Already the work was beginning.

54

The edifice, every part of which had been indexed by the technicians of different nations, had to be 'cut up' into sections, sometimes stone by stone, so as to transport it to another site where it would be reconstructed later. The pylon was still intact, but tubular scaffolding rose inside the interior courtyard along the peristyle and the pronaos. Workmen did balancing acts at the height of the capitals. Everywhere people were measuring, marking dimensions. Pathways had been specially made in the thick mud which still covered the ground. They were not adequate for the traffic and did not always lead to places suitable for photography. You had to walk knee deep in the mud. I reached the village. On the rocky slopes several houses were already abandoned. The embedded plates which formerly decorated their façades had been removed. Others, on the other hand, had been freshly limewashed as if nothing had happened, or was going to happen. Children greeted us with *guten Tag* or 'good afternoon'. This

55

56

peaceful, silent, discreet people had nothing in common with the vehement Barabras of our explorers. No one begged for baksheesh, we were far from the insistent beggars of Lower Egypt... Down below, the teams were bustling about. The home of Mandulis would leave what remained of his ancient landscape. The landscape itself, that of age-old Talmis, would disappear beneath the waters. In the shade of the little mosque old men intoned verses from the Koran.

5

I did not leave Kalabsha without going to see, for the last time, as a last pleasure, the temple's major figure: the Isis who opens the procession of gods towards the king, on the wall of the ambulatory.

56

Who would deny her beauty? She rises sinuously, to be sure, but so erect that the horns of her headdress are made to flare out in contrast, splay upwards and outwards. Following her, Horus and Mandulis walk deliberately with long strides. Her dress of wing-quills is crossed on her legs and diagonal on her hips sheathing her as if she is hobbled, forced to take short steps – the steps of a dove or a bird-soul, if you prefer it. She does not move forward. She rises. Like the sceptre in her hand, she is the stalk of a plant.

Squeezed by her girdle and brace, her nursing-mother's breast, which would sag otherwise, is lifted, with the nipple in its exact centre. It follows the curve and the horizontal of the shoulders, repeats them. We discover a skilful play of curves and uprights. Between the necklace and the top of the head a circle is adumbrated, and prolonged by the profile of the face and the wing of the bird: the disc between the horns achieves a circle. The wig on the left falls straight down over the arc of the necklace, into the axis of the body, but contained between two parallel oblique lines. However there is nothing in this image to equal the contrast between the two arms. The left arm falls rigidly, as if the heavy weight of the *ankh* was stretching or even numbing it. The outside line of the right arm is bent at a gentle angle, but the inside line is curved, a happy curve which echoes the curves of the plaits behind her shoulder.

Along the length of the body the sheath seems less a lattice of scales than bubbles rising in a vase as narrow as a vein, the movement of sap, a slow ascending force. And the navel appears on a youthful stomach, veiled by a wing.

Her headdress is a vulture, the diadem of queens. The slightly negroid profile matches her hidden inner feelings. It gives nothing away, except for the mouth whose lips tremble slightly, trying to hide a smile, trying not to betray some secret irony.

The first encounter with Ramesses II

◂ 58

59

61

62

In winter the road follows the edge of the river so closely that the water beats against it. In summer, during the three months of low water, the same little stony track is suspended on the side of the cliff. It passes above the temple of Kalabsha, then describes a curve. On the other side, if you walk north, a *shaduf,* the well of Egypt, greets you with its raised arm. It is kept very busy, when the water is adjacent, the children working it seriously or for fun. When the water is far off, it looks lonely in the rubble, with its conterweight of earth cracked like the mud of the bank. At this point the track dominates rocks with smooth sides, cleanly cut up into sheer walls, sliced, you would say, with a knife. These are the ancient quarries from which were extracted the materials used for the construction of the temple. At their feet, the cracked mud extends to the Nile.

The path climbs, passes a few houses, turns. This time we are on the other slope of the promontory. Below us opens the *khor,* the sanded up mouth of Wadi Kalabsha. A few yards farther on, on the edge of the path, two stone uprights decorated with reliefs form a very narrow door, hardly wide enough for two men together. This is the temple of Beit el Wali.

57

Less than a quarter of an hour's walk has taken us from the building at Kalabsha to this sanctuary hidden in the rocks, or if you prefer it, from the Graeco-Roman period so close to us to the antique Egypt of the great Pharaohs. In other words a leap in time of about thirteen centuries.

The first meeting with Ramesses II. A modest stage on the route which climbs to the supreme affirmation of his omnipotence at Abu Simbel. A turnstile at the entrance to the royal road of his glory southwards.

Once past the entrance pillars, you enter a long entrance hall cut into the cliff, but open to the sky. (Formerly it was covered – with slabs under Ramesses – but then with bricks on a framework when the Christians turned it into a church.) The side walls to left and right (south and north) bear many reliefs, broken up by fractures and crevices. We do not stop, for we shall return to them. Three doors open in front of us.

They give onto two halls hollowed out of the rock, as *speoi* (the temple, with an external corridor, is a hemi-speos). The first one extends crossways in front of us. It seems to close in all the more because two heavy columns, mounted on a projecting base and terminating in an abacus which scarcely protrudes beyond the shaft, impose their mass which is out of proportion with the relative narrowness of the place. Protodoric, they are incised with twenty flutes, but they bear four broad vertical bands covered with inscriptions. Niches have been made in the rear wall, on either side of the opening which leads to the second hall. In both of them the king is seated between two divinities. On the left, Isis and Horus sit at his sides; on the right, Khnum, the potter, who modelled the egg from which all life was to spring, and Anukis, goddess of the island of Siheil. Although they are damaged and broken, these sculptures still have a certain 'presence' which confers its religious character on the hall.

61

60

This character is accentuated by the paintings which still cover a very superficial relief, on the stucco with which the walls were lined. The tones are still not completely effaced. They show the king serving the gods. On the left, he offers a statuette of Maat, goddess of justice and balance, to Amun-Re. On the right, he offers wine to Khnum and Satis, goddess of Elephantine. So the walls and ceiling of this room were covered with colours which must have created a luxurious atmosphere in the little rock temple. Similar paintings decorated the second hall, narrower in depth, which houses three effigies in a niche. They have vanished today. Let us console ourselves at least with the beautiful reliefs on the uprights of the narrow door leading to this 'Holy of holies'.

60

62

The speos formed the religious part of the temple. In it the king sacrificed to the deities. Outside in the vestibule he sacrificed men and they honoured him as master and god. This time the bas-reliefs illustrate the sovereign's doughty deeds. On the south wall he conquers the peoples of the south. His campaigns against the Ethiopians, the peoples of the land of Kush, are related. Mounted in his chariot, he crushes them beneath his horses' hooves. Panic seizes the enemy. This is also expressed in a less magniloquent scene: a young man runs into a village beneath some palm trees, as if to warn his mother, busy about her domestic tasks, of the approach of the conqueror. Close by, one of the wounded enemy calls for help from his own side. The relief ends with the king's victory. He accepts the tribute of the conquered on a dais. Suddenly, Upper Nubia, far away Africa itself and the regions beyond the Second Cataract are evoked, represented by the gifts brought in token of submission. Here are wild beasts and domestic animals: panthers, monkeys, a giraffe, ostriches, cows with broad horns. Here are men: negro slaves in chains, a mother who, rather oddly, is bringing two children in a basket on her back. Here are precious wares: skins, woods, rare objects, weapons. Here are ebony, ivory. And gold. On the upper register, the governor of Nubia receives it in the name of his lord.

58

63

63, 59

The north wall shows the victories over the peoples of the north, the Tehennu (Libyans), the Asiatics and Syrians. Battle scenes: the king is about to kill the warriors he seizes by the hair, he tramples some Asiatics underfoot. Elsewhere he assaults a fortress, and one of his sons breaks in the gate with an axe. Some officers lead towards him enemies who are surrendering. Lastly, Ramesses II,

63 ►

مبروك البيت
يا عريس

58 on his throne, appears as master of the battles. In another picture, a lion lies beside him, image of his power, since the lion is 'he who devours his enemies'.

These highly animated reliefs are lightly incised in the stone. When the Nubian sun strikes the sandstone it gives off a blinding reflection, and the reliefs are sometimes difficult to read by the light of day alone because of their lack of emphasis. When they are lit suitably with reflectors, they are accentuated by shadows, and display their graphic qualities, their movement, their freedom. They often show an interest in the familiar aspects of life, a rather rare characteristic in the art of their time. Is that why some authorities prefer them to the monumental reliefs of Abu Simbel? Even if this opinion is not shared, they are not to be looked on as a 'sketch', a schema which was to be developed and enlarged elsewhere. The work exists in its own right. It does not require a comparative judgment. But we must not forget that the reliefs were painted. In 1826 a workman called Joseph Bonomi went to Beit el Wali to make casts there for an amateur enthusiast. Those casts are in the British Museum today. And they have been painted, using notes taken at the time as a guide. As for the original walls they will be cut up and transferred, together with the naos.
A religious and martial complex, such is the temple where the glory of Ramesses is manifested for the first time on the rocks of Nubia.

◄ 64

Gold and the spirit

◄ 66

67

72

Since the discovery by Howard Carter in 1922 of the hypogeum of the secretive king Tutankhamun and his priceless treasure, Egypt has been the land of gold to many people. Which of us, during a stay at Luxor or while working at Thebes, has not met a dreamer convinced he will find a sumptuous tomb miraculously spared by looters? This conviction was already held in antiquity. The kings of Babylon believed that gold was mixed with 'the dust of the roads' on the banks of the Nile. Pharaoh himself had a more precise knowledge of his resources.

He knew that the incomparable metal was not easily extracted in the mines of the east and south-east, mines, incidentally, which were allocated to him as his personal property. Requirements were large; gold had to be imported. It was brought from the land of Punt (present-day Somaliland and Eritrea). And Egypt imagined this region to be as others imagined Egypt: with gold so abundant that the shackles of prisoners and slaves were forged of it. As we see the dream of Francesco Orellana is eternal, and the lieutenant of Pizzarro had distant precursors. To tell the truth, the material value which we attribute to gold today (and which the Pharaohs had already attributed to it) is the result of such a constant degradation of its symbolical and spiritual worth that the latter no longer emerges, except among the alchemists.

To the king of Egypt, gold was one of the means of his temporal power. He rewarded his ministers and captains with it, used it to win alliances and exacted it in tribute from the conquered peoples. Nevertheless, gold still kept a deep mythical and mystical significance. It was the skin of Re. In other words the flesh of the sun itself, its brilliance justifying the resemblance. When he adorned himself with gold, the king was clothed in the light which illuminates the earth. The metal alone deified him. He was 'Horus of Gold'. There was nothing in common with the ingots of the metal stowed away in the vaults of our banks.

Gold gave its meaning to the obelisk erected in front of the temple. It covered the terminal pyramidion as a reminder that originally the rising Sun, according to the ancient solar religions, settled on raised stones. We think of the Place de la Concorde and the Piazza del Popolo.

Not subject to deterioration and imperishable, gold must have been easily connected with the concept of eternal life. It was the active symbol of eternity, transmitting it to the dead who wore it. Jewels, ornaments and gold objects in the tombs were not merely a last show of ostentation. If they testified to the dead man's wealth, still more they manifested the assurance of immortality bestowed by the metal. The less favoured social classes confined themselves to gilding the funerary mask. Among the poor the colour yellow replaced it. Solar and funerary, gold, then, was substantial, in the real sense of the word.

Egypt could not do without it. Nubia supplied a very large part of the necessary gold, whether it was imposed on the Nubians as tribute, or came from working the mines. On the west bank, about 68 miles from Aswan, near the village of Kubban, there are the remains of a fortress which dominated and protected the track of the Wadi Alaqi. The gold-bearing deposits which were reached by this route were some 37 miles away in the interior. The fortress was very ancient; it certainly dated from the Middle Empire, but it was always garrisoned. An inscription which was discovered proclaimed an order by Ramesses II for the digging of a well. The Romans, in their turn, maintained troops in this little citadel from which came the gold of the desert.

The whole countryside was of strategic importance. It had its temple on the west bank, near the town of Pi Selqît, the Pselkis of the Greeks. Today it is the temple of Dakka.

65

2

Undoubtedly you should approach – soon we shall say: should have approached – Dakka in the early morning. A grey castle, as elementary as those which children leave on beaches at night, stood out from the ochres and pinks of the dawn. One of the first rays of light infiltrated the edge of the eastern expanses, moved swiftly like a lighthouse beam, suddenly illuminating the building which appeared as a surprise to us: the façade of the pylon remained in the nocturnal shadow and only the side bordering the river was lit up, contrary to what one would have expected.

66, 67

Why was the temple built like this, from north to south, on the axis of Egypt? Apart from Philae, the other buildings in Nubia face the rising sun; the light follows the sacred line which goes from portal to sanctuary. At Dakka the two towers of the pylon are unfaithful to the symbol: they no longer represent the two primordial hills between which the Sun was born every morning. If we look at its clear profile, the temple appears to be split, cut by a fault which separates the pylon from the rest of the construction. The simple reason for this is the collapse, then the disappearance, of the two enclosing walls. Nothing is left to connect the forepart with the courtyard, the pronaos is open. Thus two simple volumes succeed each other in the now golden light. And how golden it is! As if to remind us that this was the temple of the region of gold.

In summer a broad expanse of verdant land extends westwards, up to the cliffs where the houses of the village have sought refuge. Here, in this plain, the cavalry and legionaries of Petronius, third prefect of Rome in Nubia, met the Ethiopians of Queen Candace (we should say of the Candaki, for it was a title, not a surname) and conquered them for the first time in 23 B.C. The temple had already been reconstructed by the Nubian king Arq-Amon, the Ergamenes of

73

the Greeks, whose shadow we have already met upstream at Debod.

This Ergamenes found an enthusiastic friend in the person of Jean-Jacques Ampère. Listen to the nineteenth-century traveller. 'Here is a monument from several epochs. I neglect all that dates from the Ptolemies and the Caesars, and concentrate on the inscriptions which refer to a king of Ethiopia called Ergamenes, of whom Diodorus Siculus speaks... Ergamenes interests me! I like this Ethiopian king contemporary with the first Ptolemies who, undoubtedly illuminated by Greek philosophy (the Greek physiognomy of his name may lead us to think that it was of Greek origin), dared to rise against the Egyptian priesthood. This king, called on by the priests to die in accordance with their wishes, refused to obey and exterminated them.'

In fact it appears that something of that kind did happen. At least, if we believe Diodorus, Arq-Amon refused to accept the custom of the priests of Amon at Meroë, who demanded that the king put an end to his days when they thought fit to replace him. Still according to the Greek historian, Arq-Amon reversed the situation and it was the priests who were killed, for the sovereign cut off their heads with his own hands.

3

With proportions which are correct and pleasing to the eye, the pylon of Dakka, facing north, preceded by an avenue (dromos), presents a handsome unadorned mass. 66 On the south face, two small symmetrical entrance gates give access to the interior. Three successive rooms are then disclosed. Seen from the front, when you arrive, the building is harmonious, noble and serene.

As soon as you enter the courtyard (the disappearance of the enclosing walls to west and east makes it open to the air on two sides) you are in front of the portico of the pronaos. 69 Two engaged columns, the intercolumnar walls and the general design give it great charm. As soon as you approach the threshold, the perspective of rooms opens up. Your look penetrates up to the sanctuary where the stone tabernacle still stands. 70 When you walk through the suite of three rooms, the modifications and enlargements from the reconstruction of Arq-Amon to the Roman works are revealed. The temple seduces you by a sort of radiance which is also mysterious, in spite of restoration works which are sometimes crude and the bad condition of certain parts.

The Egyptologist Pierre Gilbert sums up this impression justly. He sees it as a model of the Egyptian temple. I quote: 'It is an edifice which announces sacredness by the power and elevation of the façade. The passer-by is warned to rid himself of daily preoccupations. He enters a courtyard whose enclosure excludes all sign of the normal world except the sky. The passer-by would hesitate to go any further. From the threshold of the temple proper he saw a series of rooms diminishing in size which concentrated his attention at the far end on the tabernacle, in which the statue of the god was hidden. This mystery was favourable to the gradual preparation for worship which this architectural design inspired... The temple of Dakka, the epitome of this type of lay-out, demonstrates it clearly. With little sculpture and well preserved, it is one of the best reminders of what the over-all design of the beautiful buildings of the great period essentially was.'

As we know, the decoration of the building was not completed. The damage caused by the weather and the annual submersion is so great that in many places the reliefs only remain in the form of plaques. However the pillars of the portico on the façade of the pronaos are decorated with important pictures. 72, 73 In them we see Ptolemy Euergetes sacrificing to various deities, while on the lowest register there is a procession of sacred figures in which a beautiful Nile god appears.

71 The vegetable decoration and the offerings evoke an abundance, a rich fertility, a profusion which inevitably contrasts with the abstract horizon against which the temple stands today. Elsewhere interesting fragments remain, frequently embedded, alas, in the cement used in rebuilding. The reliefs are still more recent in the second sanctuary, built in the time of Augustus, but they show careful workmanship, especially in the depiction of the offering which the king makes to Isis and Horus. It is an academic scene, but well engraved.

On the jamb of the door which opens onto the halls of the sanctuary there is an image

74 which is unforgettable: the picture of the little Anukis, goddess of the First Cataract, regent of the island of Siheil. Admittedly she has none of the grandeur or the graphic beauty of the Isis of Kalabsha. She could not vie with her, nor with the Anukis we shall see at Abu Simbel, the admirable companion of Nefertari. This is only a 'detail', a none too confident engraving, but its charm is touching. The right hand holds a very thin tall cane which terminates in a papyrus umbel, vanished today owing to a stone fracture. The left hand clasps the sign of life. On her head an unwieldy head-dress fans out into a bunch of feathers. On the other side of the altar is the Ptolemy whose homage she receives. All the gold of Nubia for a smile from the little Anukis! She was 'she who pours the cool water'. We imagine her playing with her sacred animal, the gazelle.

4

Arq-Amon, reconstructor of the temple, was brought up at Alexandria. Undoubtedly he studied in the great city where Hellenistic cuture shone. Is it presumptuous to suppose that he acquired a taste for the humanities, even philosophy, there? His conduct with regard to the priests of Amun at Meroë indicates that he had a strong mind, breaking with restrictive religious traditions. We should like to think that the Nubian king enjoyed consecrating the new building to the ancient deity who presided over intellectual exercises, the great Thoth, vizier of Re, secretary of the gods.

Scribes of all ages, here is your master! Commend yourself to him and to his wife Seshat, goddess of writing! An astronomer, he established the calendar. A calculator, he knew figures. Clerk, you will meet him at the moment of psychostasis, when your soul is weighed. Inventor of hieroglyphics, he is the 'Prince of Books'. Lord of language, he confers on the word his active force, his magical virtue – and that is why he is also a magician.

How could he help being? Poets, the god of writing knows the Selenian spells! Protector and guardian of the moon, he is sometimes identified with it. In what guise do you want him to appear? Here he is cynocephalus, a grave baboon who meditates, seated, hand on knee, an old monkey who can be taught nothing of the divine grimaces. More elegantly, he manifests himself as an ibis, running or walking, his long beak curved back in a lunar crescent, and most often his stilt-bird's head finishes off a man's body. The god Thoth helps the wielders of the pen, the makers of signs and the kings who are also accountable (or ought to be) for their people! At Dakka, on the wall of the pylon gate, Pharaoh presents him with an offering.

But this is not the place where we should look for a lofty image of the 'civiliser of the divine society'. Let us reserve our devotion for the wall of the Ramesseum at Thebes, where Thoth is inscribed as the very effigy of creative intelligence and magic.

Be that as it may, at the gates of the route to the land of gold, the temple of Dakka thus honoured language, writing, mathematics and the knowledge of Time – and their powers.

A change of tack

So far we had gone upstream steadily without too much beating about, but, in our haste to reach Dakka, we had sailed by sites which deserved a stop. It was not our intention to rush past them. Suddenly we were in the mood of those feluccas of the Nubian Nile. They come and go, pass from one bank to the other, either to take advantage of the wind, or to find water with better fishing. Such caprices give you the pleasant feeling that there is no hurry, that time is at your disposal, the hours no longer following the same continuous thread.

Let us go about. Let us go down stream again. Here is Gerf Hussein, on the west bank.

76

Ramesses II had his second Nubian speos hollowed out of the cliff. In the open air, the temple was preceded by a courtyard with a portico, a pylon, a dromos (with two rows of sphinxes) which led to a quay. What remains of it all? Outside, two heavy columns lacking in charm, as if swollen by a sort of elephantiasis, and seven very thick pillars (there used to be eight) on which rest the remains of strangely conceived royal statues. Confronted with these colossi one hesitates to make a judgment. Are they like the man advertising Michelin tyres or the robots of science fiction?

The temple was dedicated to Ptah. 'Author of the universe, father of all beings', Sainte-Fare Garnot tells us, 'he reigned over all those whose role is to create: quarrymen, sculptors, metal workers,...' He protected craftsmen and artists. We should like to know how he judged the men who carved the stone of his temple as they did... Are we being too harsh? We may imagine that the work was undertaken by a viceroy of Nubia, anxious to please his sovereign. Clearly the faithful servant only had local man power at his disposal. He had to make

75

76

77

do with it. Anyway the important thing was to show the king's strength.
Let us enter the pronaos hollowed out of the rock. Eight effigies of Ramesses are backed by eight supporting pilasters. Their style is much better, although they are still closer to the colossal than to true grandeur. They are extremely tall (27 feet 11 inches) and represent the king as Osiris. Some of them are more 'elaborate'. The king's face has received greater care. It must be admitted that in the semi-darkness these statues have a certain massive energy. The smile of Ramesses plays on his lips. They even have a life of their own. Let us add that they have 'had their faces washed' by the Service of Antiquities. All very necessary, for the rock halls had been used as dwelling caves and the fires lit in them had covered the stones with a layer of soot.

75

A vestibule opens at the far end of the pronaos and leads to the sanctuary. Four divinities reigned there: Ptah, Ptah-Tatjenen (hating the world), Hathor and Ramesses. Here again the group has regained some of its original colours. But we must retrace our steps and look at the speos from the entrance. These Osirian pillars and this arrangement foretell Abu Simbel. It is like a rough draft of it. What will be saved of Gerf Hussein? Not the whole, for that is impossible and perhaps not worth while. Only details will be removed. And that is a pity for Gerf Hussein would have served as a point of comparison for a better judgment of the great temple in the south.

If we go down the river again, the heaviness of the external parts of the building emphasises the 'decadent' lightness of the small edifice at Dendur. From the mountain, quite close to the water, it shows us first a rectangular building whose rear is slightly embedded in the rock, then a fine entrance gate and lastly a sort of subfoundation which is both terrace and jetty. The façade of the pronaos has two columns with elegant capitals. Reliefs almost cover the walls of the central building and are rather overdone. This group of buildings dating from the Roman period – the emperor Augustus is officiating on the walls of the gate – was devoted to the worship of two local divinities, Pedesi and Pihor. The two young Nubians – two brothers, it appears – had drowned in the Nile. This tragic end had served to deify them. At first a chapel was consecrated to them. It was hollowed out of the rock behind the naos. But this little speos was not enough. It was transformed into a temple and pilgrims flocked to it.

77

Does the touching memory of the two dead youths heighten our appreciation of the elegance of Dendur? In any case Ramesses owes us a return match. He is going to give it us, so let us embark for Wadi es Sebui...

The lions and the sand

◂ 83

84

85

86 ►

◄ 87

88

90

91

◂ 89

'... It is, without contradiction, the worst work of the period of Ramesses the Great; the stones of the building are poorly adjusted, the gaps between them were filled with cement on which the decorative sculptures, which are mediocrely enough executed, were continued...'

Such is the judgment of Champollion in the *Lettres d'Egypte et de Nubie,* on the temple of Wadi es Sebui.

Such words, emanating from such an authority, should preclude all discussion... However we must be allowed to disagree with this harsh judgment. We have a soft spot for the third hemispeos which Ramesses II had erected and hollowed out in Nubia, 3,200 years ago, perhaps in the last days of his reign, through the intermediary of his viceroy Setau.

The celebrated Egyptologist Adolf Erman assures us that the narrowness of the valley forced the constructors of the Nubian temples to give up the vast traditional open-air buildings. They had to resort to the expedient which, precisely in the time of Ramesses, had become the rule for the great royal tombs: the excavation of rocks and mountainous spurs[1]. This thesis, unconvincing in itself, is scarcely justified by Wadi es Sebui. The temple there was happily sited at a point where the valley broadens out, on the west bank. 79

To the east, on the other hand, massifs with a pleasing pattern and gentle profile stand out. This is a landscape, a 'framework' not without charm. And already we begin to grieve... What will remain of Wadi es Sebui after the coming rise in the level of the water? The external temple buildings are obviously in too poor a state to be saved; they are too fragile, made of sandstone which is too powdery to be transported easily. Perhaps only the speos will escape the final submersion. Its transfer is being studied. The bas-reliefs at least will be cut up and displaced. 93

[1] *Die Religion der Aegypter.*

◄ 92

But the whole – monument and landscape, monument *in* the landscape, harmony of natural lines and man-made lines – will be no more. Thus the *genius loci* will disappear. Of course we feel the same regret about all the archaeological sites in Nubia; nevertheless it is inevitably more painful here than elsewhere.

The rock part of the temple – pronaos, treasure halls and sanctuary – was hollowed out in a spur set some distance from the river. The rest is all external: dromos, first pylon, courtyard bordered to south and north by a portico, second pylon, hypostyle hall. In fact the original structure was more complete: a large pylon wall preceded by two colossi and a sphinx prevented anyone from seeing from outside what can be seen today. However when you have passed the badly ruined Roman temple of El Maharraqah downstream, the silhouette alone of the building at Wadi es Sebui announces a grandeur, a nobility, which assert themselves and compel recognition the closer you come to it.

Its distance from the banks and the distance (about 93 miles) separating it from Aswan have spared it from being flooded every year. It could be visited summer and winter. At the period of high water, it is duplicated by an exact reflection in the mirror of a reach isolated by a tongue of land – and we saw it like that, for the first time, the simple symmetry of its façade accentuated by the inverted image. When the waters withdraw, you first have to cross the brittle shell of cracked mud to reach it, then the sand dunes which precede and surround it, dunes marked with prints of the small feet of insects and animals, and sometimes the light furrow of a snake.

80

79

The sand in the wind has pumiced the big reliefs on the pylon on which it is difficult today to make out the engraved images of the king sacrificing. Steps lead to a flagged terrace which borders this façade like a quay. There, on pedestals, stood four monumental statues of Ramesses, more than nineteen feet high. Two of them have disappeared without a fragment being recovered. The one on the south side remains in the traditional walking attitude, left leg forward, a powerful haughty mass, although deprived of his royal head-dress. To his left, sculptured in the same block, the effigy of a princess performs the same movement. On the north side of the pylon, another colossus rests in a sloping position on the stone, his legs broken, taken away. On his left he holds a sceptre which terminates in a falcon head topped with the solar disc and the *uraeus*. The *shent,* separated from the head, rests beside the body. His face turned towards the sky, Ramesses here is like a recumbent figure on a tomb perpetuated in his power.

81

81, 82

We do not leave the sovereign when we enter the square court which opens behind the pylon. To right and left on the pillars of the two side porticoes are statues of Ramesses as Osiris. Massive figures, but nevertheless free of that elementary heaviness which made the figures at Gerf Hussein look almost like caricatures. The majority of the heads have been destroyed, all of them are very badly damaged, but, below the crossed signs of the whip and the hook, symbols of power, they acquire from their very wounds a character, an expression which Ramesside art often lacks.

86

92

The inscriptions describe the temple as *Per Amun,* the house of Amun. However this 'god of the State' – we shall revert to this later on – shares the edifice with other deities exhibited on the reliefs on the walls of the rock section of the temple. Amun himself is 'associated' with Re, the Solar god, and worshipped under the 'solarised' form of Amun-Re. For his part, Re here is Re-Harmakhis, 'Horus of the Horizon'. Around these composite deities the temple contains other simpler reliefs. A relief in the pronaos, sheltered from the sun, has preserved much of its original colour. In spite of mutilations we can make out two

89

93 ►

goddesses seated one behind the other. The one on the right, wearing the *shent,* with reddish flesh, dressed in a yellow, red and blue costume, is an incarnation of water: Tefnut. On the left, her face and body coloured yellow, dressed in a long sheath of scales, her throat bare is Nekhbet, she who reigns over the regions of the south, protector of the king and the rivers in the sand. If we use our imagination, this fragment of a long register gives us an idea of what the interior polychromatic colouring of the building must have been like.

Several other pictures represent the sacrifices of Ramesses to various divinities. Sometimes they have a rather fragile line, but they lack neither decision nor mastery – in 'the offering of white bread' for example. A large relief shows the sovereign burning incense and making a libation. In front of him, Nekhbet, Tefnut and Onuris, warrior god, succeed each other from left to right. Ramesses has found a place between Tefnut and Onuris. Thus the living god honours himself in his immortal and deified form. This is one of the major themes of the decoration of the temple. Pharaoh is not *in front* of the gods. He is among them. He is god.

88

87

Wadi es Sebui, the valley of lions. That is what the Arabs called the place where Ramesses proclaimed the wholly divine character of his strength. Be reassured! These lions are no other than the stone sphinxes which guard the central avenue. Jean-Jaques Ampère, that worthy traveller, praised them magniloquently: 'A propos of the lions of Essebouah (sic), placed on both sides to form a stone avenue (too much of a good thing!) leading up to the palace of Ramesses, I would like to say a word on the role of lions in the architecture of the Egyptians and some other peoples... We shall see that this animal had its justification in the hieroglyphical system... The lion or lion's head is a hieroglyphic which expresses vigilance because, it is said, this animal sleeps with its eyes open. In my view, it is for this reason that the lions are often placed at the entrance or approaches to Egyptian monuments. At Dakka two lions are sculptured on both sides of a door which probably led into the treasury...' At least our itinerant writer does justice to the Egyptian sphinxes. They have often been confounded with their Grecian homonym, whose reputation is unfortunate. These sphinxes on the banks of the Nile do not devour travellers. They are satisfied to be the symbols of royal power, a power which they protect with their divine strength.

◂ 94

78

In Nubia, only the temple of Wadi es Sebui has preserved its sphinxes. In winter the majority disappear, but some of them are beyond the high water mark of the flood. In summer, they rest on the sand. Some have human faces. Others are in the likeness of the sacred falcon of Horus; they wear the royal crown and protect between their paws an effigy of the sovereign upright against their breast. Some rare examples have scarcely suffered from the weather. Others, possibly more moving, are furrowed, broken, mutilated, remains which are sometimes unrecognisable.

93

83, 90-91

94

We shall always remember one face, ravaged, scored and cut in half. Flush with the sand which has devoured it, it is the eternal *skull,* for ever rising from the soil; it is ancient death and its rictus – but also the sign of that which neither the wind, nor the sands stirred by it, ever succeed in totally destroying.

84

Ramesses and the Apostle

ΠΕΤΡΟΥ
ΑΠΟϹ
ΤΟΛΟΥ

96

The present-day visitor who enters the court of the temple at Wadi es Sebui and makes his way to the hypostyle suddenly gets a rather unpleasant surprise.

The lofty noble portal opening onto the inside halls has been disfigured. Small twin doors with semi-circular blind arcades have been constructed and inserted into its lower part. Thus they form two low entrances which force you to lower your head when passing through them.

85

In order to instal these orifices, the builders did not hesitate to cut into the primitive stone uprights, especially the right-hand one, regardless of the symmetry. Above the blind arcades, some filling-in shows that the upper part of the portal was possibly filled in up to the lintel at one time. Curiously enough, embrasures, which would be more in keeping with some Roman hall, have been added to the Pharaonic building. In fact it is a strange graft. A staircase with gentle broad steps led to the portal – or, more exactly, to the raised platform which preceded it. It has suffered a similar fate: a central division cuts it into two modest flights, each leading to one of the two doors. Such are the first obvious signs of a modification which took place in the sixth century A.D. when the temple of Ramesses became a Christian church. Undoubtedly out of respect for the decencies, the faithful separated into two processions before entering the house of God, men on one side, women on the other. This would explain the division and the construction of two doors. The lofty opening, made for a god-king and proud priests, was no longer suitable for simple believers who looked on humility as the first virtue.

The superimposition of the new cult on the old one is felt again in the interior. As the temple was laid out from east to west, the Christians had to erect in the pillared hall a brick apse facing east, in which they put their altar. In this way the pagan building was 'turned round' inside. In this nave, they partially destroyed the pillars on which the Pharaoh had figured as Osiris. The impious reliefs on the walls were covered with a coat of white-wash and divine images were painted on them, among others that of Christ and the Apostles, and that of the Cross and the skull, symbolic of the Passion on Golgotha. Elsewhere, on a pillar, the royal ceremonial of Ramesses is interrupted to make way for a radiant archangel.

Yet we must visit the sanctuary to see the most curious mixture of iconographies. There, in a niche in the *cella,* the statue of the king sat between representations, also sculptured in the rock, of the two divinities to whom the temple was consecrated. The Christians broke these idols and removed them. So the internal surface of the recess was empty. In it, almost in majesty, they painted a beautiful holy figure, his head naively and generously haloed. With his feet on the level of the flat surface on which the ancient simulacra rested, he holds a monumental key which would identify him, even if an inscription in Greek characters did not make it quite clear that he is the apostle Peter.

95

Nevertheless the other walls of this sacred place still retain their former decoration. The result is a pleasant confrontation. On either side of the niche Pharaoh in person makes an offering of flowers... to St. Peter! Above the latter, as if on a sort of tympanum, is the solar boat, seat of the government of the Universe! Amun is enthroned in a chapel inside it, listening to a discourse pronounced by Thoth, his vizier. On the right, three baboons in single file make the same gesture of greeting: the gesture they reserved for the Sun, father of Egypt, when he rose on the horizon in the morning. St. Peter, who is not at all scared, but good-humoured if anything, seems to be on a family visit to this pantheon whose members are showering attentions on him.

We know that the temple of Wadi es Sebui was not the only one to receive a pious baptism. Other Pharaonic buildings were transformed into churches or chapels and new symbols imposed on them: Philae in 557. Dendur in 559 and Beit el Wali, for example.

From the point of view of the history of art alone, this period is of great interest. The Christians did not limit themselves to adapting the ancient buildings to their faith; they constructed new ones which met the requirements of their cult. These buildings were given decorations which show the activity of a 'veritable Nubian school of painting', an original group although influenced by the rules of Byzantium. We already find proofs of it at Wadi es Sebui, but Professor Michalowski's Polish archaeological expedition has exhumed from the sand the beautiful frescoes of a church built on the foundations of a temple of Pharaoh Tuthmosis III at Faras, opposite present-day Wadi Halfa, on the existing frontier between Egypt and the Sudan. Elsewhere, other evidence confirms the importance of this religious painting. As for the monuments – especially the church *extra muros* of the citadel of Ibrim – they aroused the admiration of the Arab conquerors. The public's attention has been almost exclusively drawn to the Nubia of the Pharaohs and that is quite understandable. In the campaign for saving the threatened monuments, it was necessary to emphasise the buildings which would appeal most directly to the imagination. This was to the detriment of Christian Nubia. Yet it deserves a long study of its own, a more general and lengthier publication of the result of the excavations undertaken before the inundation which is going to cover ancient Nobatia. When the waters rise, many Christian remains will disappear. Thus what remains of a not exclusively Egyptian history will be destroyed. The traces of an adventure which prolonged the adventure of the western faith for so long will be effaced.

The cemetery near Aniba

99

◄ 98

100

Ramesses II's passion for buildings was so obvious that certain high officials devoted themselves to satisfying it in order to prove their zeal and reap their reward. This was the case with the viceroys of Nubia, one of them, Setau, in particular, whose foundations and inscriptions also witness to a naive desire to attract favourable attention to himself. Unfortunately this Setau does not seem to have been endowed with fastidious taste. He did not insist on perfection. He preferred quantity to quality, output to finished work. His first concern was to build extensively and fast. In fact, to do him justice, he lacked artists worthy of the name, for they were needed for the great works of the reign, for architectural undertakings which called for mastery. Undoubtedly the construction of a complex like Abu Simbel must have mobilised the most skilful labour. Sometimes Setau had to be satisfied with hacks, leaving the work of the sculptor to rough carvers. Others besides him encountered similar difficulties. They explain the defects of many Nubian buildings.

The temple of Gerf Hussein, as we pointed out, suffered from the heaviness of its proportions and from its statues being too massive. It evoked the colossal rather than grandeur, which happens when grandeur is sought for its own sake.

Similar errors are found in the speos at Derr. This great temple, hollowed out of a rock on the right bank for Ramesses, was the object of a special visit by Champollion in 1829. In it the Egyptologist discovered the image of the lion, the Pharaoh's favourite animal, among the martial reliefs; he drew the conclusion that these wild beasts were taking part in the battle. A highly controversial interpretation! The lion, left to his own devices and recovering his savage instincts, would have been dangerous to both sides in a battle, just as Hannibal's elephants were a menace, often turning on the Carthaginian troops in their fury so that they had to be destroyed in the middle of the fray. It is preferable to look on the wild beast as an executioner to whom the prisoners were delivered and more surely as a symbol of the king's strength and majesty.

The temple at Derr has provoked harsh criticism. Breasted, who studied it in 1902, pronounces this sentence: 'There is no better graphic evidence of the decline of the provincial arts under Ramesses II.' Derr is not an example of a 'colonial' style, but rather of a 'colonialist' architecture. Here again stone was intended to impose the power of the Master, the weight of his omnipresence, on countries which were not over reliable.

In other times this power did not exclude refinement. The temple of Amada, some five miles downstream, forms a contrast. Yet its construction was not prompted by different motives. Moreover one of the two great stelae it contained exalts the exploits of Amunhotep II, considered as a sort of Herculean deity. We are told of his exploits during the crushing of a revolt in Syria. He brought back as prisoners seven chiefs who were suspended from the prow of his ship. Six were put to death on the walls of Thebes, but the seventh was deported to the region of the Fourth Cataract, then executed in front of the fort at Napata. Without any doubt it was a stern warning to the peoples of Upper Nubia.

The building at Amada was the work of Tuthmosis III (–1504 –1450) and his son Amunhotep II (–1450 –1425?). It was given an additional vestibule by their successor Tuthmosis IV (–1425? –1408). The two first-named kings gave it a general lay-out which made it a sort of adumbration of those temples surrounded by colonnades which the Greeks went on building until they achieved perfection.

99

That is not its only interest. Built in the 18th dynasty, in the first period of the New Kingdom, it benefited by the care which was then given to mural images. In Christiane Desroches-Noblecourt's view, its bas-reliefs are 'of great purity'. Leslie Greener, in his vivid *High Dam over Nubia,* notes that these reliefs belong to a veritable Egyptian renaissance; their quality, according to the American author, cannot be found elsewhere. Breasted declared in 1906, when he could admire a building which was still well preserved: 'The marvellous reliefs are by a hand full of delicacy and taste, with exquisite and accurate colouring... It is astonishing that such a beautiful sanctuary is not more appreciated, for even at Thebes you would find nothing better.'

100

Similar merits can be found in the small nearby speos of Ellesyia, also built under Tuthmosis III. If we observe that Derr and Amada are situated almost opposite each other on the two banks of the river, how can we fail to draw a historical and artistic lesson? Here at Amada, strength and art harmonise. At Derr there is a divorce between them and decadence is already foretold.

It seems as if the force necessary for the seizure of these regions by Egypt suddenly materialised from the bare rock.

Just beyond the village of Aniba an imperious spur stands out then advances into the river, and soon on the east bank a rugged, abrupt, almost perpendicular cliff rises up. On its top you soon make out the remains of a group of buildings which embattle it, sometimes mixed up with stones which look like ruins. There, on its pedestal, about 130 feet above the river, is the citadel of Kasr Ibrim.

98

A citadel which acted as an observation post for several centuries! Perhaps there was already a garrison stationed there during the Ancient Kingdom in the time of Chephren. Like the Egyptians, the Romans recognised its strategic importance. They built certain parts of their own defensive system with materials borrowed from their predecessors.

When Nubia became Christian, a town sheltered behind the walls and a basilica was built which aroused the admiration even of Arab travellers. But in 1173 as the result of a rebellion by the Nubians who ravaged Aswan and penetrated into Upper Egypt, the Sultan Salahuddin, better known in the west under the name of Saladin, ordered his brother Shams el Daulah to pacify Lower Nubia. The Moslem took the town of Ibrim, destroyed it, deported the surviving population, but preserved the defences. In modern times the bastion was still strong enough for the Mamelukes to seek refuge there when Bonaparte's troops advanced to Aswan, about 143 miles downstream. Lastly the British kept an outpost there for a long time. So this castle dominating the Nile was one of the most important fortresses established on the river route to Africa, the most important between the first two cataracts, along with Buhen, where we shall soon find ourselves.

Near the base of the cliff of Ibrim, a few yards above the water level, are the entrances to five small caves. Comparatively hard to get at, they were recently considered to be tombs, but in fact they were chapels decorated with bas-reliefs of some interest. In the first one Nehi, governor of Nubia, can be seen bringing the tribute of the peoples of the south to Tuthmosis III. The second was dedicated to Ramesses II by the viceroy Setau whom we already know well. In fact these scenes entitle us to believe that the high officials of the region liked to give themselves good marks for their good and faithful services, in spite of the difficulties encountered, especially in levying tribute.

From the top of Ibrim you can see on the other bank, downstream, the very place where the city of Maam, capital of Lower Nubia, stood in Pharaonic times. Where are the palaces and the buildings which witnessed to the power and semi-independence of the viceroys? Today – but ought I not to write 'yesterday'? – a village extends its low ochre walls on the sandy ground and scatters its houses in a burning space: it is Aniba. One arcaded building contains a few services: the post-office, the police, for Aniba is still 'capital' of the province. Solider, but dilapidated houses, with peeling whitewashed walls are the homes of political opponents who have been exiled to this remote corner... How could I help remembering Aniba? During my first expedition in 1960 my comrade Michel Mitrani and I wanted to film and photograph the teams working on the excavation site. The officer who accompanied us as censor – a decent fellow, by the way – said it was strictly prohibited. The reason? It was simple. The fellaheen employed on this work went barefoot, clad only in an old gallibiya. Taking pictures of them would be to expose their poverty to the West. I tried to explain to our censor that French navvies would undoubtedly also be wearing tattered clothes if they had to shift sand in a temperature of 104°F. It was no use. We had come up against a reaction common among the underdeveloped peoples, a perfectly intelligible reaction, of course, which shows their dignity.

During the night the officer ordered the crew of our small boat to leave Aniba, afraid that our desire to take photographs would revive the next day. A fruitless discussion resulted and grew into argument. Soon I saw only one solution. I straddled the handrail and let myself drop into a lighter moored alongside the boat. Mitrani followed suit, soon followed by a third comrade. A violent altercation broke out between the officer, who ordered us to re-embark, and us, the three rebels.

It must have been one in the morning. The noise of the words exchanged finally woke the commissioner of the local police from his dreams. We saw him arrive, grumbling loudly, accompanied by two assistants. These representatives of the law threatened us with penalties for nocturnal disturbance of the peace on the banks of the Nile, then not knowing what to do, put off their decision until the morrow in order to sleep on it. As far as we were concerned the battle was already won, since the boat was immobilised. The next day we telephoned the authorities at Cairo. We had a long wait, but it was not in vain. The services of the Ministry of Culture smoothed out the difficulties. In any case Michel Mitrani, profiting by the absence of our censor, who never left me or the telephone, filmed what he wanted to film! And the delay enabled us to rejoin Professor Abu Bakr who was working 'in the field' at some distance from Aniba. You will have guessed that it was the site which had caused the comic interlude of the previous night. The field where the scholar had pitched his tent climbed gently from the river to the first rocks of the desert. It seemed to be turned over as if after a battle. Numerous holes gaped in it. Coming closer, we saw that their shade contained strangely broken skeletons. Some still wore shreds of cloth, the majority were naked. The sand was mingled with their black hair. They had no wrappings. The heat of Nubia had dried the flesh from their bones, ensuring them this protection in the secrecy of the soil until the day when this deposit of antique humanity saw the light.

An astonishing resurrection after hundreds of centuries, but how many similar cemeteries does Nubia hide in its soil? Cemeteries which are unknown to us and are going to disappear beneath the waters of the Nile? Nothing still remains of the palaces of ancient Maam and only the Tomb of Pennut, Ramesses IV's manager of quarries and temples, about two miles from Aniba, recalls the importance of the ancient governors. The bones of an arm emerged from one excavation. The hand, a fleshless talon, still had a ring on one finger and was contracted on the ground as if to retain it. Some fellaheen, in close single file, handed baskets full of excavated material from one to another. They worked to the 'Song of the High Dam', with a drum beating time.

We built the pyramids,
We shall build the Sadd el Ali.
For the Sadd el Ali, let us sacrifice ourselves.
For the Sadd el Ali, let us give our soul.

Buhen

The aircraft crossed the frontier which separates Egypt from the Sudan – a theoretical frontier, for men of the same race live on either side of the line traced by governments. On the east bank a huddle of low rectangles, administrative buildings with flags, between which moved black or white dots, rare vehicles leaving a trail of dust: Wadi Halfa. Near the bank a boat made out of two boats, one of those mail-boats which carry tourists anxious to see Nubia before she dies, fellaheen travelling to look for work and a whole bestiary of donkeys, goats and camels. It is one of those boats which ply between the frontier town and Shellal, the port of Aswan, carrying travellers and emigrants.

This is already the beginning of the country which inspired the Egyptians both with unreasoning fear and justified alarm! On top of the real threat from unsubdued peoples there were legends calculated to upset them. The far side of present-day Wadi Halfa opened onto the land of Kush, the land of mysterious perils. As the ancient Greeks imagined that after passing the Pillars of Hercules one fell into the void, the men of Pharaonic times regarded the remote districts of the south as generators of monsters and creatures which resulted from the first delirium of the creation.

Does the Nile live up to the fable? It changes its appearance, frets, puckers up. Dark shiny rocks rise to the surface in increasing numbers, then islets break and divide the stream, and real islands arise, hemming in water which rushes, seethes, surges on or stagnates in reaches, as if immobile. It seems as if the river loses its depth, streams thinly over a rocky table and widens in order to spread out its liquid mass and enable it to pursue its course. The serpentine and granite reefs are now so imperious that they part the lips of the sand. They suggest the upheaval of a shield of rocks – and you understand why the Arabs have named this place Batn el Haggar, the *Belly of Stone*.

The First Cataract cannot be compared, in spite of the heavy polished rocks of Aswan, which are so powerful, and the granite accumulations which preceded them, with this Second Cataract, for that is what we are talking about. An aeroplane enables you to measure the size of the chaotic throw, its width and its extension for some twelve miles. But the altitude squashes the relief flat. The rock of Abu Sir, near Wadi Halfa, provides the best view of the bristling chaos, the confusion of blocks of stone, the water's battle against the obstacle, a battle whose noise can be heard from afar. Navigation is impossible here. Further on, once past the rapids of the cataract, it will be constantly harassed for more than 125 miles, to the point of discouraging transport. We can easily understand the Egyptians' feelings about these regions. In their eyes, the Nile suddenly met an adverse force which it tried unsuccessfully to strangle; it ceased to be a carrier. There was something like a curse there.

The enemy could not arrive by river. He made for the desert, ready for raiding, surprise attacks, invasion. So Egypt had to instal considerable defences by making use of the natural obstacle. A chain of fortresses, citadels and camps was established on the islands and heights in suitable spots.

Mirgissa, Dabnarti, Shalfak, Uronarti and many other sites show the will which already inspired the sovereigns of the Middle Kingdom (–2160 –1580). At Kumma, the Nile forces the rocky bolt which bars its way.

Two military installations, Semna East and Semna West, were built on either side of this defile. Incidentally this was where the Middle Kingdom set the limit to its extension southwards. Aerial surveys, carried out by M. Jean Vercoutter for the Service of Antiquities of the Republic of the Sudan, have enabled us to recognise the exceptional importance of this defensive system, a veritable fortified 'line' which witnesses to an obvious strategic need.

In this field, the stronghold of Buhen appears as a work so accomplished that it can rightly be called a masterpiece. Near present-day Wadi Halfa, it stood downstream from the Second Cataract, on the north bank. The site was judiciously chosen because the river became navigable again there. This is how M. Pierre Gilbert describes the role of Buhen: it must have had 'the mission of intercepting the negro troops, smugglers or deserters who had left the impractical route of the Nile for the land routes, at the moment where they started to regain the river'. The guarding of the regions of the Second Cataract was its primary responsibility. Incidentally this role was attributed to it from ancient times, since the first citadel dates to 1991 B.C., according to Professor Walter B. Emery.

Buhen was simultaneously town and fortress. What remains of the town in particular are several temples; one of them, founded in the time of Queen Hatshepsut, was surrounded with fluted columns which made a protodoric edifice of it, but Tuthmosis III, anxious to efface anything bearing the mark of Hatshepsut, destroyed this original feature and the temple was enclosed by walls. However the lay-out of the fortress is what calls for special attention.

102

It was covered by the sands for centuries, and to that fact it owes its preservation from the corroding action of the wind. Freed from their covering, thanks to Walter B. Emery, it stands out in all its fullness. We should imagine a long rectangular mass of high brick walls from which square towers project at regular intervals, assuming the aspect of massive dungeons at the north and south corners. This complex of curtain and bastions, with battlements and loopholes, dates from the first period of the 12th dynasty. Imposing though it may have been, this building later proved inadequate – undoubtedly at the time of the tragic events which accompanied the decadence of the Middle Kingdom – and an attempt was made to render it less accessible to assaults. A patrol path preceded the base of the edifice and rounded, flanking semi-turrets reinforced it still further, pierced by rows of loopholes. Sloping glacis lined this arrangement so effectively that assailants were exposed to plunging fire by the defenders. Lastly, two buildings were extended outwards from the centre of the ramparts, crossing glacis and ditches; they framed the gate, which had however to be reached by crossing a drawbridge.

103

This brief catalogue is enough to show that Buhen could stand comparison with the most formidable strongholds of our Middle Ages. The governor's palace, enclosed by the ramparts, would prove by its dimensions that the fortress was also the protected headquarters of a great administration. Perhaps it drew its revenues from a toll which its situation allowed it to levy? In that case, Buhen, martial and commercial, would justify us in applying the modern word 'complex' to it.

In liaison with the central authority, as witness a mass of the debris of papyrus 'despatches', and with other forts and redoubts, which were near enough to warn it by means of fires, Buhen seemed impregnable behind its walls. But this was not so. About 1675 B.C. it was besieged by the Kushites. After forcing the gate, they entered the interior, looting and destroying. Fire ravaged the citadel. In 1959 Walter B. Emery discovered in the ashes the carbonised bones of a horse which could be dated to 1670 B.C. by the radio-carbon method. A valuable clue! Together with war chariots, the horse was the secret weapon of the Hyksos invaders. The Egyptians, who did not know the horse, were frightened, as the American Indians were frightened when they saw the horses of the Spanish conquistadores for the first time. Then the Kushites profited by favourable circumstances – and other peoples probably helped them in their undertaking. Whatever the truth may be, they reconstructed and enlarged the fortress about a century later, under the New Kingdom.

One question arises. The Egyptians called the men of the countries which extended around and beyond the Second Cataract 'the miserable sons of Kush'. If that was a fair estimate, how do we explain the importance of Buhen? Was it not exaggerated? Was there not something excessive in the establishment of such a defensive stronghold? To tell the truth this pejorative label is contradicted by the high walls constructed to observe and dominate the disturbing spaces of the south.

103

Ramesses II

◂ 107

109

The statue of Ramesses II which came from Karnak and is preserved in the Turin Museum arouses astonishment at first sight.

5

Is this the Ramesses who decided, as soon as he was crowned king and invested with the divine power, and barely over sixteen, to become not only the restorer of the entire Egyptian hegemony, but also a warrior and builder of such stature that History, in the course of time, would exalt his acts and hold him for a major figure in the human adventure?

The polished granite shows the effigy of a young man conscious of his importance, to be sure, but nevertheless not accustomed enough to it to hold its attributes and symbols with assurance. His father, Sethos I, had associated him with many of his works, thus showing his predilection. But was not his inheritance (a controversial one: did his elder brother die or was he criminally disposed of?) inevitably premature? The body of the young Pharaoh leans slightly forward, as if still familiar with the games of childhood, and his head, one would say, is bowed under the weight of a prolonged adolescent reverie. An inward look, the cautious smile, give this face a sensitive, meditative gentleness. If the nose were not strong and aquiline, it would be flawless, more appropriate to a leader of souls than a leader of armies. This dreamy serenity will never be quite effaced, we shall find it again, but slightly modified, in the last images, on the profiles of the king charging the enemy, on the colossi of the temples, on the interior pillars where the king assumes the form of Osiris. This was how Pharaoh had to appear to men: master of himself and of circumstances, for he is Master of the Universe, the Elect of Re.

106

Let us make no mistake. This sort of 'detachment' does not contradict the ardour which Ramesses was always to devote to the exercise of power, to the satisfaction of his senses by the enjoyments and pleasures of life, to the establishment of his glory. There are few sovereigns who manifested their will to power as continuously, even as crudely, as he did. Undoubtedly in his last years he granted too much autonomy to certain officials and the ambitious priests of Amun, thus preparing a difficult future for his successors, but his despotic authority was maintained almost without wavering throughout his reign. A reign of exceptional duration, since it went on, we must remember, for sixty-seven years.

◂ 111

If we discovered any trace of effeminacy in the Turin masterpiece, the young king's first acts would disprove us. He knew the perils threatening Egypt to south, east, west and north. He saw in these perils the chance to establish his renown, and quickly too, to make the force of his arms felt, to assert himself. He took the easiest course; he won Nubia in full battle array.

The stages in his campaigns were manifestations of prestige, intended to dazzle the peoples of the distant banks. At Aniba, capital of the province, he learnt from the viceroy that plunderers from the south were terrorising the regions of the Second Cataract. His decision was taken. He organised a punitive expedition, ascended the river, fell on the enemy bands, beat them, massacred them and imposed heavy tributes on them. Too easy a victory, one might say, over hordes of negroes? Certainly, but the king at once exploited it for publicity purposes, amplifying an enterprise in which, to put it briefly, he was learning the trade of general.

This journey and the attendant battles revealed to him the need to pacify these perpetually turbulent zones definitively. He thought of establishing new fortresses, of consolidating the old ones. Still more, temples would have to be built to add to the force of arms the unconditional respect due to the divine person of the Pharaoh. Perhaps he decided during this journey on the construction of Beit el Wali, on whose walls would be depicted the processions of the peoples of the south bringing their offerings to the victorious chief, in complete

submission. Did he envisage that his colossus would compel attention, repeated four times, four times imperious and sovereign, in the place we call Abu Simbel, on the edge of his boundaries? A police operation turned the young king into Ramesses the Nubian.
Soon he was forced to deal with the threats weighing on the west, on the northern of the delta. Nothing could irritate him more. The delta was the district from which his family came. Moreover, in the eastern part, he wanted to devote his attention to creating and developing a new town, *his* town, the Pi-Ramesses which some historians locate at Qantir, others at Tanis. Thus the peoples of Libya, who had been thought relatively subdued, grew bold and aggressive again. They comprised different ethnic elements. The Hamitic Tehennu resembled the Egyptians physically but not in their way of life. Almost naked, they adorned their bodies with animals' tails and their hair with ostrich feathers. In the vast steppes of a poor country where oases were rare, they mainly drew their resources from wandering flocks and their ability to guide and convoy caravans in the desert solitudes.
With them were the quite dissimilar Temnhu, with their pale skins, red or fair hair and blue eyes, Berbers perhaps or rather Indo-European immigrants into Africa who had imposed their presence on the native population. Do we not also speak of the Akuasch, in whom we must recognise the Achaeans from the other side of the sea, driven from the country of their birth? These peoples were restless: migrations took place under the pressure of the mass of men who were displaced and scattered over the east of the Mediterranean basin. In addition the lands of the delta were fertile and desirable. Was that the only reason why a group of these Libyan peoples seized some villages on the western fringe and occupied them? They quartered themselves there, as if surprised at their own audacity in defying the power of Egypt.
The incident took place in the fourth year of Ramesses' reign. The king did not give the invaders time to settle. His army dislodged the 'barbarians' who were already growing soft among the delights of more favoured lands. However he spared those known as Shardana. He took them back into captivity and then enrolled them in his ranks, for he valued their bravery in battle and their courage. The Shardanian mercenaries were to constitute his shock troops. Ramesses was to reserve them for the most dangerous actions.
The battles in Nubia and those in Libya (which some historians consider doubtful) belonged to the infancy of the art. They were excellent preparatory exercises, they enabled the young chief to hold a march-past of prisoners at Thebes and so prove that in his case valour did not wait on age. The real test awaited him east of the isthmus where the elusive and plundering Bedouin had no scruples about seizing the forts with which the Egyptians protected the route to Palestine – and still more in the regions of Palestine and Syria over which the influence and protectorate of the Pharaoh had become precarious, in spite of the former campaigns of Sethos I, while the pressure of Kheta, the kingdom of the Hittites, the main enemy, constantly increased.
In 1294 Ramesses undertook a journey which led him from the delta to Byblos, by way of Gaza, Jaffa, Acre, Tyre, Sidon and Beirut. If we except a detour into the interior, as far as Megiddo and Beisan near Jordan, he followed the coast. Prudence? Undoubtedly. In the case of an unexpected attack which his inadequate escort would have been unable to master, it was easy to summon the Egyptian ships which cruised off the coast and re-embark.
Was this an expedition? By no means, but rather, if you like, a round of visits to allies and military headquarters, a journey to gain information. Ramesses wanted to judge on the spot the fidelity of the petty Phoenician princes, to assure himself of their attitude in

the event of a conflict. On the other hand if he crossed the Nahr el Kelb and reached Byblos, was this not to breathe the air of the enemy from which he was separated only by the land of the Amorites? The Hittites were not far away. The ambitious young commander dreamt of establishing his glory by defeating the people his predecessors had never really been able to conquer. To break the enemy's power definitively, re-establish Egypt's authority over Northern Syria, even to restore the Egyptian Empire in Asia, such was the plan which necessity, the national interest and personal pride all inspired.

The Hittite king, Muwatallish, was equally driven by pride. He already knew what war was from having fought against Sethos I. He estimated that his successor was still inexperienced. His tactical position was good. For a long time his emissaries had been demoralising the Pharaoh's allies, trying to win them over or at least incite them to adopt an advantageous 'neutralism'. The citadel of Kadesh, on the Orontes, formed a powerful barrier protecting the north; it served as an advance post housing a large garrison. He had to take advantage of such favourable circumstances. The prince of the Amorites had just chosen alliance with Egypt, abandoning his treaty with the Hittites. This was the chance Muwatallish had waited for. He broke the truce established in the time of Sethos. War began again.

Once again Ramesses took the road to Palestine. He had to face a powerful coalition. Voluntarily or by force, his adversary had obtained the collaboration of twenty peoples. The Hittite army has been estimated at about 13,000 men and 3,500 chariots. The Egyptian was careless, so full was he of his own superiority and his contempt for the peoples of the north. Choosing the offensive, he made his way by forced marches to the valley of the Orontes and Kadesh. If he seized the fortress, he thought, Asia Minor would open up to him, there would be nothing to stop his victorious march. No hostile army came out to seek battle. He divided his own army into four legions placed under the protection of the four great gods Amun, Re, Ptah and Seth. They followed each other at varying distances. Ramesses did not group them, he scarcely gave any credit to the strategic qualities of the Hittites. Besides, they seemed to have abandoned the country. He advanced without finding any major engagements, as on a conquered land, and so arrived before Kadesh. The Pharaoh was accompanied only by his guards, some Shardanian mercenaries and the legion of Amun. True, the citadel was in a state of defence, but only small patrols defended its approaches. Ramesses smiled. He thought the enemy was afraid. Two Bedouin spies, captured by his soldiers and then questioned, confirmed him in this opinion: they wanted to join the Egyptian ranks, they assured him, because they were ashamed of this Muwatallish who had taken refuge in the north on the approach of the terrifying great Pharaoh. Ramesses and his officers did not doubt their words. The horses were unharnessed from the chariots, arms were laid down. Shields were stuck into the soil. Everyone prepared to take the rest which the unexpected circumstances allowed. Ramesses withdrew to his tent. On the western bank of the Orontes, the Egyptian camp relaxed.

Sudden shouts shattered the calm. They were the strident cries by Muwatallish's warriors as they took the assault. Far from having gone to the north, they had hidden themselves in the environs of the fortress. The Hittite king had expected that his enemy, deceived by the mendacious story of his two Bedouin emissaries, would fall into the trap and abandon his vigilance.

From all sides, as if springing from the soil, the troops of Muwatallish rushed on the Egyptians and encircled them. Chariots knocked down the soldiers who tried to grab their arms, turned tents over on their occupants, crushed shields and men beneath their wheels. Some resistance took shape among the Egyptians, but it seemed to be drowned in the confusion and panic. Already the rout had begun. Never had lack of foresight and presumption been paid for so dearly. It was all up with the Egyptians, unless a miracle...

Ramesses reacted. He cursed the runaways and tried to rally round him the few men who had not panicked, the intrepid Shardana, a few soldiers of his guard, the legion of Amun. And he addressed a prayer of supplication to Amun: 'I call on thee, O my father...' He knew that it was in vain to count on prompt help from the other legions, they were too far behind, but he despatched messengers to them. Could he hold on until the nearest one arrived? The young king understood that his fate was at stake, that it was better to perish than to be taken and conquered. He mounted his chariot and ordered his driver Menna to charge on his enemies to the east, on the flank where he had observed that they were less numerous, inconvenienced by the river. Was he alone in this charge, as legend has it?

109, 110

His assault was almost suicidal, but his fury discountenanced his enemies and revived the ardour of his own men, who imitated him. The stupefied Hittites surged back to the Orontes, tried to cross and drowned in it. Muwatallish had forces in reserve. This episode did not worry him. He hurled in a thousand new chariots to finish with the handful of resisters, now grouped around his adversary. This time Ramesses seemed to be lost. His own driver begged him to flee. Fortunately, his luck turned. Behind, the attackers, surprised by their easy victory, were solely occupied with the rich booty they were collecting and quarrelling over, without trying to take the Egyptians in the rear. Finally a crack corps and then the Ptah legion arrived, thanks to the time won by the Pharaoh. The equilibrium of the forces was not re-established, but the enemy lost confidence and retreated. The soldiers of Ramesses remained masters of the field of battle.

Was this a victory? Egyptian propaganda claimed that it was and spread the news. Poets exalted it. Sculptors engraved it on stone. Even History was deceived – until the day when Hittite tablets were discovered proclaiming with equal firmness the triumph of Muwatallish! True, the severely tested forces of the Pharaoh had not been wiped out. On the other hand, Kadesh remained intact. On that point Ramesses' undertaking had suffered a setback. He willingly accepted the truce proposed by Muwatallish: it enabled him to take his army back to Egypt without the honour of his arms being compromised. In fact the costly war finished in a 'draw', but Ramesses was skilful enough to impute the errors committed to his entourage and to highlight his personal heroism. From now on he would be the king who, alone in the fray, abandoned by everyone, averted disaster without regard for his own life.

The rivalry of the powers, however, was not interrupted. Revolts in Palestine instigated by the Hittites soon forced the Pharaoh to intervene there, in the seventh year of his reign. But the obstinate Muwatallish died. His succession caused discord, dividing the enemy into rival clans and weakening them. Ramesses took advantage of the favourable circumstances. After the taking of Dapur (where he further gave countenance to his heroic legend by fighting without his breastplate) he could claim to be the victor. King Khattushilish signed peace. It was the prelude to a reconciliation. The Hittites were still more worried about the threat hanging over them from Assyria. So they proposed a treaty of alliance with Egypt. Finally Ramesses, bereft of his favourite wife Nefertari, married Khattushilish's daughter in 1264. An inscription at Abu Simbel will tell us in what conditions this marriage took place. It was, of course, for the greater glory

112 ►

of the Egyptian, who did not scruple to put himself forward as the protector of Kheta. Was Ramesses a strategist? He used every method to ensure that his contemporaries were in no doubt about his martial qualities. He was able to use the walls of the monuments he commissioned to advertise his real or fictitious triumphs. We have related the military history of his long reign because it helps us to understand the conventions and the iconography of an art wholly devoted to his praise. The battle of Kadesh, the taking of Dapur, the campaigns in Nubia, Libya, Palestine and Syria, we shall see them, as he wished them to be seen, at Karnak, Thebes, Beit el Wali and Abu Simbel.

A constructor he was, but with a sort of violent passion. He showed this passion as soon as he acceded to the throne. He was to complete works which others did not know how to, or could not, finish. Was it filial piety alone which led him to put the finishing touches to his father's funerary temple? In any case, he wanted his name to figure beside that of Sethos. He restored the ancient monuments of his ancestors, on condition that his own surpassed them. He wanted the tomb that was hollowed out for him to be bigger, deeper, richer and more abundantly equipped. His colossus, in his own funerary temple – the Ramesseum – was to dominate the site of Thebes. It was he who was to finish the giant hypostyle hall at Karnak. At Luxor he erected obelisks and added the buildings of a new courtyard which he filled with his effigies. There was no end to his works as a builder. He visited the sites personally, supervising the work and boasted that he improved the lot of the workmen. Wars provided him with man power: prisoners were employed on the most arduous tasks.

◂105,107, 111

We observe in him a sort of pathetic desire to leave a trace behind, to conciliate the favour of the gods for the eternity which awaited him. He was not satisfied with building monuments to his glory, to his religious fervour. He did not hesitate to have the names of his predecessors effaced and shamelessly replaced by his own. The list of these usurpations is a long one. He was so preoccupied with this scandalous procedure that he took steps which would spare him from being its victim, should occasion arise. When the smallest of the obelisks at Luxor was cut down to be transported to France, it was noticed that the name of Ramesses appeared on the base. Even if usurpers had engraved their cartouche on the four faces, the monolith would have secretly remained his property, the offering of the builder. His name! His name! Seldom has what we nowadays call the cult of the personality been carried so far.

◂113

It is difficult for a policy of grandeur to avoid grandiloquence. In order to conform to his political designs and illustrate them, the architecture of Ramesses often yields to the grandiose. Its aim is not so much proportion as effect – but the effect, we must admit, is undeniable. The hero of Kadesh did not want to establish an original mode of expression. Above all he wanted to strike the imagination by the number of his buildings. So building had to take place fast, without worrying too much about perfection of detail. Thus the bas-relief proper became less frequent: it called for scooping out the stone around the figures, making them stand out. These operations slowed down the spectacular rhythm of public works. So he resorted to incised relief, which was quicker. Simple designs incised in the stone sometimes replaced the traditional manner which had produced masterpieces so recently, in the reign of Sethos.

104

Yet can we deny that Egyptian art, in the reign of Ramesses II, exhibits images, rhythms and groups of buildings of undeniable force? That would be to forget the exceptional successes, in which loftiness and sensitivity, mass and rhythm, actuality and symbol all harmonise.

And if all we had was Abu Simbel.

Abu Simbel

114 ►

15 ►►

6 ►►►

LE CARO
1875
1875
PITET

The slow ascent of the river did not lead to Buhen and the fortresses of the Second Cataract, nor to the 'belly of stone', beyond which the land of Kush began in the eddies, but to the site downstream whose modern name has sounded like vibrating brass in the fanfares of modern news and journalism: Abu Simbel, the 'cymbal' word which punctuates in quasi-Wagnerian fashion the drama of condemned Nubia. Philae has not its sonorous attraction; it lends itself less to visual simplification, in spite of the silhouette of its kiosk of Trajan. Abu Simbel has taken precedence over all the other places, excessively so, and the reader must not be impatient with our re-examination of certain familiar images or the enthusiastic judgments it produces.

Let us confess that during our first mission impatience led us to reach it as soon as possible, even when it meant by-passing other sites. We had got the Nubian captain of our little boat to agree to navigate by night. It had taken long negotiations to persuade him: he was afraid that in the dark he might hit one of the palm trees covered by the high waters of winter. Moreover his fear was well founded. Just after midnight we were awakened by the hull scraping on a tree trunk. The *Taouaft* came to a halt, its propeller caught in the palms invisible on the surface. It was a miracle that no serious damage interrupted our voyage. We freed the vessel, then went back to our cabins. A few hours later, in the morning, we tied up to the bank. The porthole formed a copper halo round the first picture of Abu Simbel.

What strikes you, even before the two temples compel your attention, is the sand, the heavy outflow of sand which crosses the crest of the cliff and pours down to the river, as if the western desert was putting forward an advance guard. On either side, the wall of sandstone falls in a steep slope. To the north, it approaches the water: the façade of the small temple almost borders the

115

◄ 119

stream, but to the south the rock is set back leaving the large square in front of the great sanctuary. Thus a bay opens towards the east and the hills of the east bank.
This place is going to disappear. Now there is no doubt that it was chosen for its character. Even before Ramesses it housed a religious foundation – we find Middle Kingdom inscriptions there – but the Pharaoh's undertaking harmonised with the site. A man carved his image in the rock there, on the edge of the moving water and the shapeless desert. He gambled on himself, in his possible accession to eternity. Abu Simbel is not a humble place.

114

However, the sand nearly triumphed over it. Driven by the wind, it climbed for centuries like a flood-tide along the proud colossi until it covered and drowned them. They would certainly have foundered if the Swiss traveller J. L. Burckhardt had not discovered them in circumstances which we had better leave him to relate: '...I had visited all the antiquities of Abu Simbel and I was preparing to re-ascend the sandy ravine in the same way as I had descended it. By a lucky chance I walked a little farther on, southwards, and my eyes lighted on what is still visible of the four immense colossal statues, carved in the rock at a distance of some six hundred yards!
The news of the discovery spread and the romance of their resurrection, as M. Louis Christophe has related it, began. Three years later, Giovanni Belzoni, acting for the British Consul-General in Egypt, tried to remove the sand from the façade of the great temple, but he came up against the opposition of the Nubians, who had already wrecked the efforts of his predecessors, Caillaud and Drovetti. He returned in 1817 with a strong expedition. During the first few days, the natives agreed to remove the sand, then they withdrew, abandoning Belzoni and his companions. They decided to continue the task with their own hands. There were five of them, in addition to Belzoni: a representative of the Consul, two English captains, a Turkish soldier and a Greek cook! They shovelled away for ten hours a day at a temperature of 111.2°F, living solely on maize and water. In the course of twenty-seven days' work they freed the top of the portal, slid inside the temple and discovered the speos by the light of their torches in an inferno of heat. Then they returned to Cairo, having performed a great service to archaeology.
In fact it was another expedition which cleared the south colossus and a part of its neighbour in 1818–1819: then it was known that the effigies of Ramesses were seated, not upright. The fame of Abu Simbel was established. Travellers succeeded each other, important ones too, since they included Champollion, Burton and Lepsius. In 1850 Maxime du Camp took Gustave Flaubert there and brought back some daguerreotypes which were fortunately added to a collection of drawings and abstracts already made. As for the author of *Madame Bovary,* his impressions when confronted by the great temple, which he gives in his *Voyage en Orient,* are surprising, to say the least! The noise of the bats reminded him of the ticking of a country clock. Then he thought 'of the Normandy farms in summer, when everybody is in the fields, about three o'clock in the afternoon'! Should we prefer the enthusiastic piety of Miss Amelia B. Edwards? The celebrated and scholarly traveller arrived (in 1874, if I am not mistaken) in front of the sanctuary and observed that the face of one colossus was badly spotted with white. It was the remains of the plaster used by Joseph Bonomi – a personage we have already met at Beit el Wali – to take casts. Miss Amelia could not bear such sacrilege. She had a scaffolding erected, then ordered the men of her team to climb up and clean the august face. Unfortunately the plaster had seeped into the hollows of the stone and

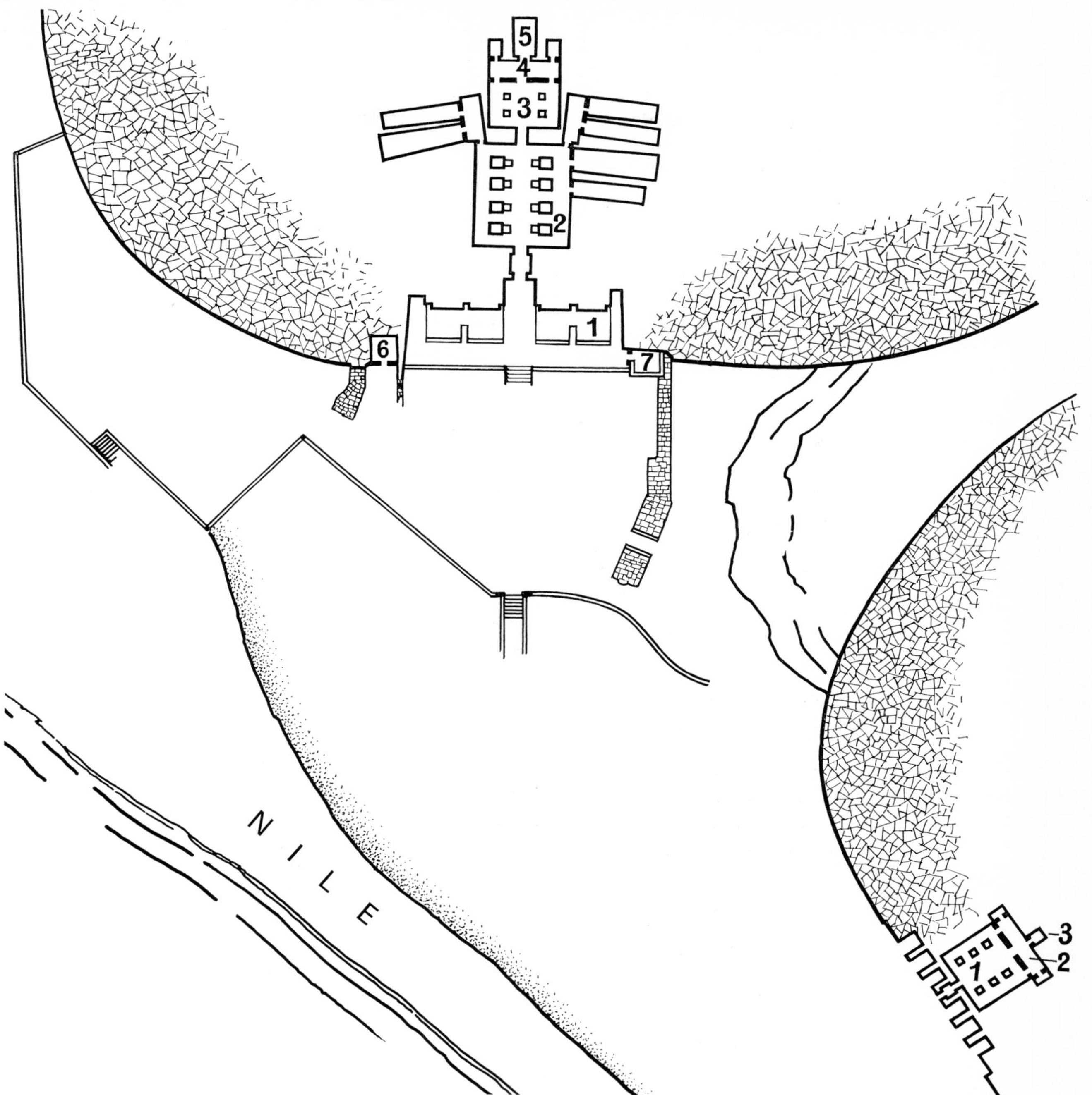

SITE OF ABU SIMBEL

Plan of the great temple: 1. Terrace and colossi. 2. Pronaos. Eight Osirian pillars, eight lateral halls open into this pronaos (store-rooms for religious objects and offerings). 3. Vestibule. 4. Second vestibule. 5. Sanctuary. 6. Chapel in the rock (speos). 7. Outside chapel.

Plan of small temple: 1. Naos with six Hathoric pillars. 2. Vestibule. 3. Sanctuary.

washing was not enough. Then Miss Amelia ordered her cook to make bowls of black coffee – and the patches of plaster were dyed with this beverage.
Fact or fiction? At any rate it was in 1909–1910 that Barsanti, architect of the Service of Antiquities, took advantage of the first increase in the height of the Aswan dam and the rise of the waters to work on the great temple. He cleared the terrace, extracted the statues decorating it and freed the north chapel. He completed the 'desanding' of the whole lay-out.

The rebirth of Abu Simbel, as we have been able to see it, took nearly a century.

2

The façade of the great sanctuary of Abu Simbel, so frequently reproduced, has become familiar[1]. We are accustomed from pictures to this trapeze and the four colossi which are inscribed in its opening. It, too, forms part of that iconography which modern techniques drill into us at second-hand. However if we stand in front of the work, freeing ourselves from the habit and feeling of *déjà vu,* the element of wager it represents grows again, the plastic adventure rediscovers its novelty.

116

A break with tradition. The double trapeze which forms the usual pylon of the Egyptian temple could have been hollowed out of the sandstone as a piece of *trompe l'œil.* It was decided that there would be none of that: a single trapeze is represented in the rocky mass. In the same way, the effigies of the king were not sculptured separately, then placed in front of the façade, as is the case at Luxor, as had been the case with the colossi of Amunhotep III (known as Memnon) at Thebes. Did the problem of transport arise in these remote regions? The explanation is unsatisfactory. If these four giant statues were sculptured in the rock itself, inside a single trapeze, there were good reasons for it. Grouped like this in twos on either side of the central axis, they give the façade a compactness whose static energy impresses you instantly. They are not detached, they form part of the monument. They assert its absolute unity. They link what they represent with the significance of the temple. Ramesses is the temple, as the temple is Ramesses. Moreover the repetition of almost identical attitudes possesses the magic of visual rhythm, the optical equivalent of the repetition of phrases in litanies and invocations.
A figure in quadruplicate, Ramesses II is sitting in judgment. Standing, he would be more reassuring. Seated, he makes you feel as if you are appearing in court. He sets himself up as a tribunal composed, not of different judges, but of a single judge with his effigy repeated and thus endowed with ubiquity[2].
Does this mean that he threatens? Torso bared, decorated with a necklace and the pectoral engraved with the name used at his enthronement, his hands placed flat on his thighs, feet on the ground, there is nothing indicating violence in the angles of this body. The whole face, surmounted by the double crown, bordered by the *nemes* whose stiff sides fall down onto his chest, prolonged by the false beard which signifies religious office, seems beyond, *above* the events which may occur. The hint of a cautious smile reveals not only wisdom but a remote irony with regard to the world and its illusions. Here is suggested the detachment which confers a certitude of eternity, the voluntary withdrawal into the self which would prove

114

[1] Let us recall its dimensions. Width at the base: 125 feet 6 inches. Height: 105 feet 10 inches. Depth of the edifice in the rock: 208 feet 4 inches.

[2] Champollion has remarked that these colossi are *portraits* which exactly resemble the figures of the king which one can see at Memphis, Thebes and elsewhere.

124

125

RS IZARD
1834

formidable, crushing, devastating, if suddenly awakened. This is the image of a potential energy, always ready to become active again.
Thanks to this subtle serenity, the colossi of the façade possess the character which takes them out of the sphere of the massive propaganda of a despot into the sphere of art. Monumental sculpture? Architectural, if anything: the legs form a sort of colonnade, the busts and heads a sort of giant frieze. Rarely has sculpture in the round been so fused with architecture, to the point of actually being architecture.

3

Certainly the conqueror made no secret of his intentions here.
Not without reason, Ramesses imagined that these megalithic simulacra would inspire the peoples of Nubia with respect and fear. He conceived them on the grand scale. The dimensions? The colossi rise, as we know, to a height of 65 feet 7 inches. The forehead measures 1 foot 11 inches; the nose, 3 feet $2\frac{1}{2}$ inches; the ears, 3 feet 5.7 inches; the mouth, 3 feet 6.7 inches; the width of the face from ear to ear is 13 feet 8 inches.
Although their expression is peaceful, we divine the existence of an implacable power, always ready to swoop down on rebels and refractory subjects. Although they have a far-away look, just as the Pharaoh was far away in his northern capital, they nevertheless witness his constant 'presence'. The wall which surrounded the temple was low enough for the tops of the statues to be visible. They were entrusted with the role of magic guardians.
The outside of the sanctuary is entirely devoted to Ramesses. The terrace extends on either side of the central staircase which has shallow steps. Five statues decorated it on both sides, to left and right, alternating with five Horus-falcons, his symbol. The majority of these twenty sculptures, which punctuated the edge of the terrace at regular intervals, have disappeared today; some were displaced, others mutilated or crushed by blocks falling from the rock face. When it collapsed, the colossus to the south of the portal pulverised the statues at its feet. However it is not difficult to imagine this long gallery of symbols and portraits: they made up the first degree of grandeur, the most modest if you prefer it, leading up to the family statues joined to the legs of the Pharao and the colossi. Thus a graduation was established. The eye was led from the 'normal' image to the monumental one.

118

128

A strong round moulding marks the internal angles of the trapeze, demarcating the northern and southern edges of the flattened rock. The upper part of this torus frames a long hieroglyphic inscription: the ceremonial of the king, which is repeated on either side of the central axis. Above, dominated by a badly damaged gorge, the cartouches of Ramesses, flanked by two *uraei* succeed each other in an unbroken band. Ramesses! Ramesses! Before this pediment on which he commands our attention, we may ask ourselves, like a certain Egyptologist: 'Where are the gods?' And reply: 'This temple certainly seems to be consecrated to the king, to the royal entity, rather than to the gods of the Pantheon.' (Desroches-Noblecourt.)
One fact seems to contradict this: the presence of Re-Harakhti, god of the rising sun. He appears in an oblong niche, above the portal, his sparrow-hawk's head wearing the disc. He is erect; his dynamic attitude contrasts with the static colossi which surround him.

117

It was to him that the sanctuary was dedicated, for him that it was built... At least, that interpretation persisted for a long time! It was the obvious one, it harmonised with the traditions. Today, the guides hasten to point out to visitors the elements which make up the relief set into the rock: on the left, the dog-headed sceptre *User,* seen front view; on the right, what remains of a figurine of the goddess *Maât,* daughter of Re. When the name of the latter is joined to the two preceding words, a composite word is obtained: *User-Maât-Re*. Now User-Maât-Re is Ramesses II's prenomen! In other words, on the pretext of representing the god, the king is named once again. This play of shapes is equivalent to a play on words. What we have is a rebus.

On the right and left of the figure of Re-Harakhti, on the wall, we shall have noticed two symmetrical bas-reliefs: Ramesses is making an offering to the god. In his hand he holds out to him a statuette of Maât, symbol of justice and truth. How can we help thinking that he is offering it to himself? That here Ramesses II is honouring himself in his own immortality? He merges with the solar master. He is the god to whom this temple was consecrated, the 'Sun King'.

4

The interior of the sanctuary does not contradict what is asserted by the façade. Once past the portal you enter the first hall where the feeling of grandeur, created by the same means, once more takes hold of the visitor. In this speos [1], the hall is the equivalent of the courtyard in temples built in the open. In it we find the Osirian pillars which line certain sides of such courtyards, as we have seen, for example, at Wadi es Sebui, if we confine ourselves to Nubia.

128, 137

These eight statues, nearly twenty-three feet high, arranged in two rows, four to the north and four to the south, facing each other, produce an incomparable effect here. Because they are partly struck by a ray of light, because they are only illuminated by the reflection of the external light, they assume a strangeness which full daylight would deprive them of. The eight effigies are haloed, they radiate, sometimes seeming translucid, with their actual substance illuminated to the point of dissolving it. At night, in the growing shadow, they give the pronaos the aspect of a hypogeum, an entrance hall to the Other Life.

137

The variations in their luminescence, during the hours of the day, give these oblong shapes, resting against the rectangular pillars, a sort of metamorphic life. Ramesses into Osiris? Yes, but the king takes precedence over the god, political significance encroaches on the spiritual symbol. Not only has the clinging sheath of the god disappeared, but the statues on the north side wear the double crown which evokes Heliopolis, and those on the south wear the white crown of Thebes. Thus the two religious capitals of north and south are honoured with some skill. But let us leave that. The Osirian Ramesseses of this hall continue the powerful conception which inspired the colossi of the façade. There is no break in the grandeur. Moreover this double line of effigies breathes magic, their made-up eyes seem both bewitched and able to bewitch the visitor.

Numerous though the religious representations and scenes of offerings may be in this pronaos, we cannot help comparing it to a 'Gallery of Battles'! With the exception of the Osirian pillars, nothing attracts our attention more than the military reliefs which decorate the walls. They present the martial chronicle of the reign either in historical 'frescoes', or in images which exaggerate the events in order to recall the omnipotence of the god-king. Ramesses is not only 'a' victorious king: he is 'the' king who can *only* be victorious, by virtue of his origin and his essence. He fights for Egypt as commander in war, but even more he protects it as divine mediator, saving it from danger less by strategy than by thaumaturgy and charisma.

129 ▸

[1] Dimensions: 59 feet × 54 feet 8½ inches.

One would say that the vast scene which occupies the north wall of this hall belongs to the chronicle, to the annals. It is a recital in pictures of the battle of Kadesh. True, the major episode of the war against the Hittites has been described several times, in particular at Thebes, on the wall of the Ramesseum, where the conflict of chariots and soldiers is expressed in all its violence. Everything is as confused as could be, the better to emphasise the decisive intervention of the king among the chaos. Here, at Abu Simbel, the ups and downs of the battle are related on the stone. We finally manage to pick out the complicated events of the battle and arrange them in sequence. We guess that the artist was ordered to depict as much as possible. On the central band of the lower zone, Ramesses – larger than the other personages, so tall that an assistant has difficulty in raising the fan of the *flabellum* to the height of his head! – sits on his throne, holding council with his vizier and his officers; farther on his chariot, its impatient horse being mastered by a chariot-driver. On the lower band: the Pharaoh's personal bodyguard, Shardanian mercenaries, recognisable by their helmets surmounted by crescents – and this important scene: the Hittite spies being beaten with sticks to obtain confessions and information.

The allusion is obvious. These are false confessions which will fool Ramesses and make him fall into the trap laid by the enemy. Here, too, is the Egyptian army. Assured that Muwatallish is withdrawing northwards, as the spies convince them, it encamps without taking proper precautions: the relief at Abu Simbel depicts it protected by a rampart of shields, the men going about their camp duties. But, in the upper zone, hostilities are raging. Our Egyptians, surprised, fight desperately. In the centre a fortress appears: Kadesh, without any doubt, surrounded by the two arms of the Orontes. On the left, Ramesses charges, bow in hand, while the two cavalries clash. Above, near the north-east corner, the battle terminates: prisoners walk in procession before Ramesses standing in his chariot.

◂ 130

Let us refer to our earlier account of the battle of Kadesh. The relief on the north wall faithfully illustrates the official history. The whole is a muddled epic whose various parts are devoted to the king's valour. Its aim was to affirm a victory which we know quite well was questionable and often questioned. Here is a monumental example of eyewash in a kind of strip cartoon, a page of immoderate propaganda. Naturally the historian finds valuable material in it, but the aesthetician can hardly be pleased with this garrulous narrative. To our taste at least the graphic quality is continually mediocre, banal, slapdash. The figures seem to have been incised in the stone hastily, as if the artist was anxious to please and frightened to omit any of the details commissioned. It is a second-rate advertisement.

We shall not be so severe on the reliefs on the opposite wall. On the contrary it seems to us to bear some of the most energetic drawing of the Ramesside period. Below an upper register, divided into five traditional scenes of offerings, three large pictures are inscribed on this south side of the hall, all three showing masterful treatment.

To the left, on his chariot pulled by a plumed charger, Ramesses, erect, is facing the enemy. He has knotted the reins round his waist so as to have more freedom of movement. Behind him, three of his sons, also in their chariots, follow him into battle. In front of him is a citadel. Men on the towers express the despair of impotence. Others, on the ramparts, beg the imperious adversary for mercy. One of the besieged, doubtless hit by an arrow, falls from the walls. A crouching woman begs the Pharaoh for mercy with outstretched hands. In the lower corner, on the left, a shepherd drives his flock ahead of him, and also raises his arm to avert the peril. An analysis of the work is not enough to express its dramatic character. Ramesses

130

and his horse and chariot assert themselves right in the middle of it to such an extent that the rest of the composition, however important it may be, seems to be recessed. The Pharaoh himself stands out from this central group, as if he was advancing towards us, in reliefs against his surroundings. The effect has been obtained by deepening the contours of the silhouette; the darker shadow confers an optical relief, a virtual volume on the figure. We shall also notice the contrast between the almost vertical figure of the king and the Mannerist elongation of the body of his horse: this liaison between the perpendicular and the horizontal converges on the vehicle's wheel which thus 'distributes' the lines around it. The astonishing impression is that of a *static movement,* if I may so describe it. The horses, the chariots advance – and yet seem to be absolutely fixed.

On the other hand, a kind of agitation reigns in the left third. Here we are in the human sphere. These personages in the stronghold who are going to yield are human. Human, too, is the woman who is asking for pity. Only too human... this fleeing peasant with his frightened beasts. Let us consider this last relief: rarely has graphic art been able to sum up like this, in a single attitude, fright, even panic, the misery of the people in the war waged by their masters. The engraver of Abu Simbel inscribed an image for all time in this sandstone: the ideogram of every exodus.

Questions have often been asked about the second profile which duplicates the bow and the arms of the king in this relief. According to certain scholars, we should see in it a correction, a case of second thoughts on the artist's part. The carver of Abu Simbel wanted to improve his work. Is this explanation adequate? Not in our eyes. Not only lines were altered, but volumes. Moreover the decorations were already determined, nothing was left to chance in their execution, and the engraver could not indulge his personal whims. Finally these 'alterations' can be observed elsewhere in the same picture. Is there not a sort of technique of deliberate repetition here? In the view of some scholars the artist wanted to suggest the presence of the Genius of the Pharaoh, a Genius who accompanied the king in battles, inspired him, protected him and led him to victory... This theory is worth considering. However the reason for these 'echo' shapes remains conjectural. Let us merely say that they do no harm to the scene from the plastic point of view. On the contrary, they convey depth by playing the role of a cast shadow. They also evoke, deliberately or not, the movement of the bodies, kinetic energy. Ramesses appears to lean forward to left and right, the better to strike the enemy he is pursuing with his arrows. He is 'multiplied' by his audacity and his ardour.

Because it is simpler and less composite, the following relief in the centre of the south wall is all the more accomplished. The scene represents Ramesses in the act of killing a Libyan chief. This time the king is fighting on foot – man to man, on the same level as his enemy. In his right hand he brandishes a spear; in his left he grasps the arm of his adversary. The latter makes a vague gesture of supplication, flexes his knees, snaps backwards. Ramesses is astride another Libyan, a Libyan felled to the ground, dying: the Pharaoh's right foot crushes his skull. If we look at the profiles of the two conquered warriors, both express a sort of tragic fatality, impotence confronted with the young irresistible hero. Here we again find the convention of the two long files of prisoners (Asiatics to the north, Africans to the south) at the base of the colossi on the façade, on either side of the entrance. There the deliberate schematism of the bodies and faces was alleviated by volutes formed by the plants of Upper and Lower Egypt which served as the captives' bonds. On the inner picture on the south wall, the incision rejects details, anything which might soften

141

142

131 ►

132

133

◄ 134

135

◂ 138

139

141

142

C.V

its severity. The actual curves on it give way to a syncopated rhythmic design, where angles and straight lines tend to form a geometrical type of composition. Everything seems hard, acute, authoritarian. Two men are going to perish beneath the victor's blows. Three bodies confront each other in the nudity of life and death. The tragedy is stripped to its absolute essence.

The last volet of this sort of triptych follows these warlike descriptions. It is the triumphal return of the king. Ramesses, in his chariot again, parades in all the relaxed majesty of a victorious peace. His horses arch their proud necks. The familiar lion, symbol of power, accompanies the team. There are prisoners in front of the king, on two superposed registers.

The captives are offered to the gods as a sacrifice. The scene is depicted, in this first hall, on the walls which are on either side of the portal and the door leading to the sanctuary. These scenes do not belong to the chronicle alone. In spite of the details which enable us to recognise the race of the victims, the meaning of these pictures is not confined to history in the true sense of the word. They were credited with a magic power, as if the divinities, *actually* receiving the offerings, were averting danger, through the intermediary of the Pharaoh. They enter the realm of a 'magical prophylaxis' (Desroches-Noblecourt). In the temples built in the open air, such pictures unfold on the pylons, outside. In the sanctuary-cave of Abu Simbel, they could only be inscribed on the inside walls.

On the inside east wall, below the two sacrifices depicted, eight sons of the king succeed each other on the south side and nine of his daughters do likewise on the north side. The princes, with a martial air, holding the *flabellum* and making the gesture of adoration, advance with a firm tread. The princesses, as if motionless, make the same gesture, and play the sistrum, the sacred instrument of Hathor, in their left hands.

140

139

They have a restrained charm. The profile of their faces is cut into the rock, while their young bodies are moulded and curved in low relief within the broad triangle formed by a dress transparent enough to reveal the shape of their long legs. Thus the descendants of the Pharaoh are not absent from the hall of his trophies. They are there to share them. Even more: to prove his vital force.

5

The remains of painting on the reliefs and statues give us some idea how intense the colouring of the pronaos must have been originally. The ceilings of the lateral naves are starry skies. The ceiling of the central nave is decorated, between the royal legends, with a procession of large vultures whose wings spread from one edge to the other. They lead to a vestibule, then to a hall of modest dimensions which opens onto the sanctuary through three doors. The progressive lowering of the ceilings, the increasing inclination of the sun, have been harnesses to give the feeling that you are penetrating into the inner part of the mystery, towards the place where the Powers reside.

128

They are there. Their effigies have been carved in the mass of rock. Behind them, it is merely rough stone against which their four seated forms stand out. The temple finishes here, but with their mysterious look they testify to that which has neither beginning nor end. Traversing the temple is like that crossing of the nocturnal world which leads to each new day, to the permanent renaissance of the light after the voyage in the darkness. From left to right, Ptah, Amun-Re, Ramesses II and Re-Harakhti are seated. We are immediately surprised by the 'installation' of the king among the gods on an equal footing. He appears here as a god, no less than those who surround him. If we remember that Ramesses considered the three deities named above

133

as the components of a Unique Being, the fact of placing himself 'in' their triad also assumes an important meaning. The façade where the sovereign asserts himself as master, had already warned us of his intentions, but the definitive proof is given by the sanctuary: the temple of Abu Simbel is the temple of the god Ramesses.

What gave him the courage to attempt this audacious move? The experience of Amunhotep IV Akhnaten (though less ambitious) had caused troubles which Ramesses must have known about. He must have known how the State regretted it. Since this dream (admirable in itself) of Nefertiti's husband, would not the priests prove suspicious, touchy? M. Louis A. Christophe proposes an explanation which we must mention. On the site of Abu Simbel (or very close to the present-day site) was the village of Meha, where a Horus was worshipped. Ramesses particularly honoured him and then identified himself with him. Meha was far away in the south, the Horus of Meha had hardly any importance: the priests of Thebes, Heliopolis and Memphis did not react. Then Ramesses grew bolder. When the edifice hollowed out of the mountain was decorated, the secondary deity made way for the traditional gods of the pharaonic royalty – for Re-Harakhti in particular – and Ramesses, when no protest was heard, no longer distinguished himself from that god. The same process was followed for Queen Nefertari: at first she was identified with a local Hathor, venerated in the village of Ibchek, then she became identified with the great Hathor to whom the second temple at Abu Simbel would be consecrated. Unfortunately Nefertari died before attending her own deification. Ramesses himself benefited by this operation which was conducted with prudence and skill. M. Louis Christophe (*La Revue de Caire,* November 1961) sets forth the other episodes as follows: 'Originally this deification of the sovereign only applied to one of his hypostases, the one which was expressed in the prenomen or surname used at his enthronement. It was subsequently extended to his whole person and this development was expressed by a new identfication: the deity was designated, no longer by the royal prenomen, but by the name which the sovereign bore from birth... In the subsidiary halls of the temple when the name of the sovereign was followed by the epithet "the-great-god", it was not meant to indicate that he was already dead, but this was the simplest way to make it known that he had acquired all the divine qualities and prerogatives *in his lifetime.*'

The same eminent Egyptologist has devoted himself to dating the execution of the work on the great temple. According to his examination of inscriptions and reliefs, the main work was finished before the year 26 and the decoration towards the year 34 of the reign. In other words, we are led to ask ourselves whether this giant enterprise was not intended to celebrate the first thirty years' jubilee of the Pharaoh. Such a holiday, the *Sed heb,* called for a luxurious commemoration by which the king proved that he had lost nothing of his energy. Let us quote M. Louis Christophe again: 'Was not the aim of Ramesses II, aged barely fifty-five, with numerous descendants, by hollowing out of the mountain of Meha his *temple of millions of years,* to take advantage of this important event in his earthly reign (the thirty years' jubilee) to satisfy his immense pride? By identifying one of his hypostases with Horus of Meha did he not try to prolong in a new and relatively discreet direction the religious ideas of Amunhotep IV Akhnaten, without the risk of raising the Theban clergy against him, since he did it in Nubia?'

We see that the date of the works brings us back to the deification of the king: the first *Sed heb* would have enabled him to make a preliminary attempt. After which he would go further: 'On the second jubilee (in 34) *his whole person* was deified: it was the sacred boats of Ramesses II which decorated the

144

north walls of the hypostyle hall, the sanctuary and the southern chapel... A new theology was born: the king was equal to the gods while he was still on earth.'
M. Louis Christophe advances this conclusion: 'The great temple of Abu Simbel was hollowed out to ensure the deification of Ramesses II, while he was still living, on the very day when he celebrated his thirty years' jubilee, towards the 20th October of a year around 1260 B.C.'

6

Towards the 20th October? That is to say during one of the two periods in the year when, thanks to the ingenuity of the builders, the rays of the rising sun penetrated to the far end of the sanctuary and illuminated it. More precisely still: the day when these rays lit up, among all the others, the statue of the king. Let us explain.
Facing east, the façade of Abu Simbel is always exposed to the full light of the sun during the morning. From the moment when the sun passes the zenith, it enters the shade to spite the tourists brought by regular boats in the afternoon, when the colossi cease to be photogenic for lack of contrasts.
During the twelve months of the year the rising sun moves from north to south on the eastern horizon of the temple, then from south to north. So there are two periods during which the rays are too far north or too far south to cross the threshold before the sun is high, the more so because the colossi of the façade then form a screen on either side. On the other hand, during two other periods the rays of the sun can enter the hall with the Osirian pillars and strike certain parts of it successively. These periods last from 10th January to 30th March and 10th September to 30th November.
132,133, 134
The sun penetrates as far as the sanctuary totally or partially illuminating the deities in it one after the other, during two shorter
◄ 145
periods: from 10th February to 1st March and the 10th to the 30th October.
We should note that only the three solar deities (Amun, Ramesses and Re-Harakhti) then receive the rays. Ptah, in the left corner, is barely touched for a moment on the shoulder: he remains in the shade. By placing him thus out of reach of the rays it was intended to indicate his character as a funerary god, which was sometimes assimilated to Osiris. The lighting of the statues is not a chance effect. The engineers intended it to obey a plan in accordance with theology.
Twice a year, about the 20th February and the 20th October, the sun rises on the horizon in the actual axis of the temple. The three statues receive the rays directly. Ramesses is completely bathed in them. In this physical phenomenon, there is a sort of mystical encounter. How can we help thinking, with M. Christophe, that a 20th October was deliberately chosen for the thirty years' jubilee – and perhaps even for the completion of the temple? The sovereign saw himself greeted by the rising sun – by Re-Harakhti – on the same day as he was deified.
Let us leave these considerations which will appear unprofitable to some. For those who are interested in them, we mention the detailed pertinent study, full of original insights, published in *Le Courrier de l'Unesco,* in October 1962 by Mr. Jan K. van der Haagen[1].

[1] Mr. van der Haagen asks himself: 'Was the great temple at Abu Simbel an observatory?' He has observed that the orientation of the axis of the temple is connected with the appearance of a star of Orion, a constellation which the Egyptians assimilated to Osiris. So the 'tunnel' formed by the temple was useful for fixing the appearance of this star. Moreover, Mr. Van der Haagen shows that the priest officiating in the north outside chapel – a chapel to which we shall refer again later – could observe a part of the horizon between the crenels of the wall. The orientation of the small building is different from that of the terrace which it prolongs. The reason for this curious fact is suggested by Mr. Van der Haagen: the axis of the chapel is directed in such a way that the priest could see the exact point in the sky where the sun appears.

Let us imagine ourselves at Abu Simbel once more, as we once were and as we would like to be again, in the unchanged landscape, at daybreak.

The growing pallor of the sky gives the desert wastes a dark weight, but soon the Nile, reflecting the bright heights, infuses the earth with the dawn, and already the heights of the east, the last spurs pushed towards the river by the Arabic mountains, show their contours worn by sand and wind against the light. An incandescence runs along the ridges, the light crosses them, hastily, industrious. The late stars are disappearing, shells abandoned on a beach which a new high tide is going to cover.

The sun finds its way through an opening in the hills. Its oblique rays strike the top of the cliff of Abu Simbel; as the sun rises, they will descend the façade of the temple, bathing it in light. First the long upper relief is illuminated: baboons, 7 feet 6½ inches high, at one time twenty-two of them, are arranged in a frieze, the first witnesses. The cynocephaluses, (I observed it myself in negro Africa) shout and jump about when the light comes. The ancient Egyptians made them the animal emblems of the rising sun, as we have made the cock its symbol in our latitudes. They saw a dance in honour of the god in the monkeys' scampering; a hymn in their cries. Couples of divine cynocephaluses, it was thought, invited the day to return to earth by their prayers. Representing the apes on the dominant moulding, on the top of the façade which was illuminated by the first light, met the requirements of the myth. Moreover it reminded the Nubians that the monkeys formed part of the tribute exacted by the Pharaoh when they submitted to him. In addition the cartouches and ceremonial of Ramesses, situated immediately below in parallel strips, chisel out their hieroglyphs in the play light and shade which is beginning. When the sun rises in the axis of the temple or close to it, it seems to extract from the rock the central image of Re-Harakhti which dominates the portal. The god walks to meet the sun – but he is advancing towards himself, for he is the god of the rising sun, 'the sun rising on the horizon'. And as the sculpture forms a rebus of the royal prenomen, Ramesses sees himself as if enthroned by the solar force, enthroned in his divine function. The colossi are now in the conflagration and the conflagration reaches their bodies, the pedestals, the terrace and the beach of the square. Then the sun-king and the sun-god merge in the same affirmation.

7

The great temple of Abu Simbel appears to yield up its religious significance, making no attempt to conceal it. However symbols abound on it and the architecture itself expresses them. For example, the two small chapels which flank the façade to north and south deserve to be studied. The first, on the north, is in the open air: it has even been built outside the trapeze, on the side of it, but it is entered by a portal giving onto the terrace. It contained an altar decorated with four sculptures of monkeys and four obelisks, works which are in the Cairo Museum today. This chapel was intended for the morning worship of the rising sun. So it was consecrated to Re-Harakhti, to whom the left half of the great temple was devoted. The other chapel, to the south, was hollowed out of the rock. Amun was worshipped in it. And the south half of the temple was Amun's preserve.

The disparity between the two buildings reflects the characters of the two deities. Amun is the hidden god: the secrecy of an interior chapel was better suited to his title of master 'whose name is hidden'. A similar intention appears on the uprights of the door: the inscriptions on the north side are 'in clear'; on the south, they are in cipher. Thus mystery and obviousness are mixed at Abu Simbel.

◄ 148

149

◂ 150

151

As for the political importance of Abu Simbel, numerous inscriptions on the walls and the rocks nearby attest it. Officials on a mission and important personages who went there or stopped there called on the rock to bear witness to their passage and especially to their loyal intentions with regard to the deified king. Thus we read on them the acts of fidelity of the four viceroys who succeeded each other during Ramesses' long reign. The epigraphy of the site abounds in documents. We can read an important one on the south face of the cliff, near the terrace of the great temple. A bas-relief surmounts the inscription. Ramesses, on his throne, accompanied by the gods Ptah and Sutekh, welcomes a new bride, Maa-Hor-Nefrure, led towards him by her father Khattushilish, king of the Hittites – an event which we have already referred to[1]. The text on this so-called 'marriage' stela proved difficult to decipher because of the bad condition of the stone. We remember the sight we saw during a first mission in 1960: Professor Jaroslav Cerny was still studying the old text in the middle of the night, with the help of projectors whose light scooped out and clarified the characters which were eaten away. This nocturnal picture was a typical example of the work which was going on continually in the face of the threat of submersion.

Let us quote an extract from the inscription, in Professor Cerny's version, for it does not lack poetry nor grandeur:

'For years, the great king of the Hittites wrote to pacify His Majesty, but he never listened. And when they saw their country reduced to this sad state by the great wrath of the king of Egypt, the great king of the Hittites addressed himself in these words to his soldiers and notables: "Our country has long been wasting away and the wrath our lord Sutekh (the god) cherishes against us is not appeased. The sky does not send its rain down on us; all countries are our enemies and fight us all at once. Let us strip ourselves of everything we possess, beginning with my eldest daughter, and let us bear our propitiatory gifts to the good divine king (Ramesses) so that he may grant us peace and allow us to live." Then he sent off his eldest daughter, preceded by a magnificent tribute of gold, silver, base metals, countless slaves and horses, cows, goats and sheep in their tens of thousands. They brought everything in profusion.

'A messenger was detailed to say to His Majesty: "See, the great king of the Hittites has sent you his eldest daughter, with an abundant tribute of every (kind of) thing. These presents are brought to you by the great notables of the land of the Hittites and the princess of the Hittites who is at their head. Leaving behind it many mountains and difficult passes, the procession has reached thy frontiers. May it please Thy Majesty to send his army and his notables to meet it."

'He immediately sent his army and his notables to meet them (the Hittites). Then His Majesty deliberated in his heart, saying: "What is going to happen to those I have sent forth and who travel as envoys towards Syria, in these days of snow which denote winter?" Then he offered a great sacrifice to his father (the god Sutekh), whom he beseeched in these words: "The sky is in thy hands, the earth is beneath thy feet and everything thou hast commanded comes to pass. I beseech thee, do not send the cold rain and snow until the wonders thou hast destined for me arrive!" And his father Sutekh granted all his prayers: the sky was clement and during this winter there were such fine summer days that his soldiers and

[1] Sutekh: god of the eastern delta, to whom the Syrian Reshep is assimilated. According to Adolphe Erman, *op. cit.*, 'the god Sutekh is the same as the god Seth of Upper Egypt; what we have is a barbarian transcription of his name.' As regards the name of the young queen, it is already Egyptianised as a matter of course. She is 'she who sees Horus, the active force of the Sun' (Desroches-Noblecourt). Three other reproductions of the text which covers the stela are in existence. That of Abu Simbel is the best preserved.

◂ 154

notables travelled enjoyably, their limbs at ease and their hearts rejoicing.

'When the daughter of the great king of the Hittites continued her journey to Egypt, she had in her retinue the chariots and notables of His Majesty, mixed with the infantry and chariots of the Hittites, without distinction between foreign warriors and Egyptian troops. All ate and drank together, having but a single heart, like brothers, and no one sought a quarrel with his companion; peace and fraternity reigned among them according to the will of the God himself. And the great kings of all the countries they traversed were amazed and looked round, discountenanced at seeing the men of the land of the Hittites and the soldiers of the king of Egypt together.'

The inscription at Abu Simbel only partially reproduces the text drafted at the king's court, doubtless because the engraver lacked the space for it within the limits of the stela. However that may be, we observe once again Ramesses' intention of asserting his superiority. It is said that the king was delighted with this marriage as a love match, although it might have been made for purely political reasons. Nefertari, his favourite, had been dead for a long time. The Hittite princess was young. And this Pharaoh was approaching his sixtieth year.

8

Cosmic temple, official temple, strategic temple, the monument of Abu Simbel is also a family, one might almost say 'tribal', one, since the vast household of Ramesses is represented there. To left and right of each colossus, between the ankles, there are twelve statues which symbolise, as we suggested, the creative force of the king – but they bind him, the reigning god, to the world of the living, to the stuffiness of the women's quarters, to the secrecy of alcoves, to the freedom of the courtyards where the children play.

116, 119, 136

Yet the wives, daughters and sons sculptured here are only a sort of 'delegation'. In addition to the Great Royal Wife whose pre-eminence was not disputed, there were many secondary wives and then came the favourites of the harem. How many children had Ramesses II? Perhaps two hundred... Some of them died, such as the young prince Ramessu, who appears between the legs of the third colossus (we shall number the colossi from south to north; from left to right when facing them). Do we see, to the left of the first megalith, the princess Bent Anta, his eldest daughter, whom he married? The whole, restrained though it may be in comparison with reality, produces the impression of an inexhaustible fecundity. It is only fair that the queen mother Tuya should be shown twice (to the left of the second colossus and to the right of the third): she is the begetter of the begetter.

129

Our attention is inevitably drawn first to the two sculptures which advance towards us on either side of the portal, to the right of the second colossus, to the left of the third one. Here is the Great Wife at the beginning of the reign[1], Nefertari, repeated in her pure nudity.

2, 117, 122

With her, with her images, femininity resumes its rights in this Abu Simbel which seems to be devoted to male strength: a femininity in which charm and strength are allied. We are indebted to it for one of the noblest effigies in Egyptian art, on the façade of the great temple. Surrounded by the heavy wig and ornaments, here it is, the perfect equilibrium of the face where sensuality is matched by nobility. High, wide apart breasts, worthy of the most beautiful *apsaras* in India, serve as prelude to the stomach and the pelvis which already hint at walking, the movement of the two legs. The arms hanging on either side of the body follow the symmetry of the heavy coiffure. *Incessu*

[1] An honour she shared with Isis Napert. The latter died early. She is not represented in the temple.

patuit dea. The goddess is recognised by her walk.
A short distance away, on the other side of the downflow of sand, Nefertari awaits us in the small temple where she harmonises rather than identifies herself with Hathor. The monument, also hollowed out of the 47, 148, 49, 150 rock, adopts the slope of the cliff. It seems to support it with its seven massive buttresses, decorated only with large hieroglyphs. A door opens in the central buttress. Between the others, in the recess which separates them, are six statues about 33 feet high. To both right and left Ramesses stands twice over beside his wife. The princes and princesses who accompany them are beside their legs.

Where are they going, these humans whose 148 untouchable youth is eternalised in the stone? The water of the river is so close that they could easily step forward and bathe their bodies in it, spattering each other with foam and laughter. No, they are making for the sun, the rising sun, the child-sun, which is the fruit of their flesh, the Son they are going to bring into the world.
In the inside hall, two longitudinal rows of six pillars bear heads of Hathor framed with wigs with heavy falling curls, surmounted with temples whose doors open onto a 146 rearing *uraeus* prolonged by two shafts recalling the sistrum. So it is not Osiris who receives us here, but the goddess of joy, music and dancing. The whole speos is stamped with her character. Here Ramesses can appear as commissioner of offerings: the 152 gods will help a happy young man; even if he appears as a warrior chief, he is sacrificing his enemies to the young woman present, to the Nefertari who, on certain reliefs, protects him with a gesture and replaces the magic signs with her body.

Nefertari herself is given an even purer form in the reliefs on the walls. On the walls of the secret halls, she is as if elongated by the 145 chisels of an artist in love with a model whom he undoubtedly never saw, an idealised figure. Isis and Hathor surround her, making the gesture of protection above her head. Was a more simple cadence ever invented? A more intelligent simplification of gestures? Elegant hands. Subtly interpreted curves. Bodies with density, but represented with a few incised lines. Even more, the revelation of a mystery in the silence: Nefertari has become Immortal.
Elsewhere she performs the gesture of offering before Anukis, goddess of the 153, 154, 144 cataract. The profile of the latter seems familiar to us. Because an Egyptian carver, thirteen centuries B.C., already knew how to 'write' the line of a face and had full mastery of his hand as had later Piero della Francesca when 'writing' the profile of Battista Sforza, Ghirlandaio when 'writing' Giovanna Tornabuoni, and Piero di Cosimo Simonetta Vespucci's.
Thus, in the images of a young queen, the art of Abu Simbel, which some writers decry or accuse of being only the expression of megalomania, undeniably attains the domain of simple volume, pure line and of love both fragile and everlasting.

Addendum

ALPHABETICAL LIST
OF THE PRINCIPAL MONUMENTS
AND SITES

ABU ODA Speos; New Kingdom (about 1325 B.C.). Converted into a church in the Christian period. *Dismantled. Will be rebuilt on the new site of Abu Simbel.*

ABU SIMBEL Great temple of Ramesses II. Temple of Queen Nefertari. New Kingdom, 19th dynasty (thirteenth century B.C.). *Dismantled and rebuilt higher up, on the same site.* See pp. 196-255.

AKSHA 25 miles from Abu Simbel. Remains of a small temple from the period of Ramesses II dedicated to Amun. Reliefs, inscriptions, among them the enumeration of the Asian peoples conquered by the Pharaoh. *Bas-reliefs cut out and reinstalled in the gardens of Khartoum Museum.*

AMADA Temple of the New Kingdom, 18th dynasty. Remarkable decoration from the good period. *Moved 8,500 ft, raised to 210 ft.* See p. 172.

ANIBA Ancient capital of the Viceroys of Nubia. Tomb of Pennut, high official in the period of Ramesses VI. *Relocated on the new site of Amada.* Excavations by Professor Abu Bakr in the necropolis. See pp. 166-174.

BEIT EL WALI Hemispeos from the period of Ramesses II. Inscriptions, reliefs illustrating the campaigns and victories of the king. *Walls sawn up, temple transferred to the new site of Kalabsha, near Aswan.* See pp. 108-119.

BUHEN Fortress. Ruins of the temple built by Thuthmosis II and Queen Hatshepsut (—1520–1484). *Rebuilt in the open-air museum*

at Khartoum. The fortress (sun-baked bricks) cannot be saved. See p. 177.
Near Buhen, remains of an Old Kingdom town which can be dated to the 4th dynasty. This would make the Egyptian occupation of Nubia even older than had been thought; it would go back to the period of Cheops and the Great Pyramid. Another recent and very important discovery: this town had copper works.

DAKKA Built by a king of Nubia in the Graeco-Roman period. *Relocated on the new site of Wadi es Sebui.* See pp. 120-134. During the dismantling of the dromos parts of the first sanctuary, built by Tuthmosis III in honour of Horus, came to light.

DEBOD Built by a Nubian king. On the façade the Roman emperors Augustus and Tiberius are depicted among the gods. *Dismantled, transported to the island of Elephantine.* Offered by the U.A.R. in recognition of foreign aid. See pp. 83-85.

DENDUR Greco-Roman temple. Dedicated to two heroes by the Emperor Augustus. *Dismantled, transported to the island of Elephantine.* Offered by the U.A.R. in recognition of foreign aid. See page 139.

DERR Temple hollowed out during the New Kingdom, period of Ramesses II; dedicated to Re Harakhti. *Walls to be cut up.* Offered by the U.A.R. See pp. 171-172.

GEBEL CHAMS Small chapel excavated in the rock in the time of Poeri, 'Royal Son of Kush', about 1000 B.C. This prince held the high office of royal fly killer. *To be transferred to the new site of Abu Simbel.*

ELLESYIA A speos temple hollowed out in the time of Tuthmosis III (—1504–1450); *important features to be removed.* Offered by the U.A.R. with four other sanctuaries, in recognition of foreign aid. See p. 172.

EL MAHARRAQAH Graeco-Roman temple. *To be transferred.*

FARAS (East and West) Ancient capital of Nobatia. Church built on temples from the Middle Kingdom and the period of Thuthmosis III. *Important features (especially frescoes) to be removed and transported.* See pp. 164-165. The cathedral brought to light by Professor Michalowski's Polish mission contained sixty-nine paintings, some of which were super-imposed. Painted on wet or dry plaster, some of them are very large (*The Nativity* is over 13 ft high by 22 ft wide); fifty-two of these frescoes have been offered to Poland in recognition by the U.A.R.

GERF HUSSEIN New Kingdom temple, hollowed out of the sandstone under Ramesses II. Massive style, undoubtedly owing to Nubian craftsmen. See p. 136-139.

IKHMINDI Important remains of a Byzantine town. The foundation stone of the fortress was discovered in 1959.

KALABSHA Temple from the Roman period, reign of Augustus. Numerous reliefs illustrating the cult... *Dismantled, then rebuilt on a new site.* See pp. 86-107.

KASR IBRIM Chapels in the rock. Fortress from the Christian period. *Details to be cut up and transferred.* See pp. 172-173.
Important discoveries by the Egypt Exploration Society (England). Remains which go back to the 18th dynasty (1570 B.C.).
In 1963-1964 Professor Plumley of Cambridge discovered the vault of a fourteenth-century bishop here in the ruins of the biggest Christian church in Nubia. In the prelate's vestments two scrolls, one in Coptic, the other in Arabic, describe the bishop's consecration in 1372. These manuscript scrolls prove that Christianity survived the Moslem invasion in the twelfth century and

continued in Nubia until the fourteenth and fifteenth centuries.
Professor Emery's excavations at Ibrim have thrown more light on 'group X', a mysterious people who occupied Kasr Ibrim until the middle of the sixth century A.D.

KERTASSI *a)* Temple from the Roman period. *Dismantled and transported in crates to the island of Elephantine. Reassembled on the new site of Kalabsha, near Aswan.*
b) Small speos, inscriptions and busts, carved out of the rock of the quarries. See pp. 83-85.

MIRGISSA South of Buhen. Fortress; ruins of a small temple from the time of Sesostris III. See p. 177. The excavations of the French archaeological expedition (Professor Vercoutter) have made it possible to estimate the extraordinary importance of the Middle Kingdom Egyptian fortress and prove the existence of a military town. The extent of this archaeological zone is so vast that there is little hope of exploring it completely before the submersion, in spite of the great efforts which have been made.

PHILAE Group of temples from several periods, especially the 30th dynasty (—378–341 B.C.). Constructions continued under the Ptolemies, finished during the Roman period (first to second century A.D.). To be preserved *in situ*. See pp. 44-79.

SEMNA EAST (KUMMA) Fortress. Temple. *Relocated at Khartoum.* Built under Thuthmosis III. It may be that men built the most ancient dam in history at the height of this site, taking advantage of the narrowing of the valley, and the rocks. See p. 178.

SEMNA WEST Advanced fortress of the southern frontier under the Middle Kingdom. Temple. *Relocated at Khartoum.* See p. 178.

SERRA Fortress. Remains of a town.

TAFA Temple from the Ptolemaic period. *Dismantled.* Offered by the U.A.R. in recognition of foreign aid. See p. 83-85.

WADI ES SEBUI Period: 19th dynasty, Ramesses II. Temple, partly external, partly hollowed out of the rock. An avenue *(dromos),* lined by sphinxes, leads to the pylon. *Relocated on new site.* See pp. 140-165.

To this list should be added other archaeological sites where studies and excavations have taken place, such as Gebel Adda, Akba, Argin, Khor Dehmit, Dorgonarti, Wadi Allaki, Ballana, Qoustul, Sabagoura, Sheikh Daoud, Tomas, Sayat Korosko, El Madiq, Mainarti, etc.

Longitudinal section of the Great Temple of Abu Simbel, as it will be rebuilt. In black: concrete framework. Hatched: sandstone slabs carefully sawn and cut up (façade and ceiling of the internal halls). These slabs are to be cemented to the framework. It is planned to build a hill on top of the whole. ►

FURTHER DETAILS ABOUT THE HIGH DAM

A sluice has been planned by the Soviet engineers. According to Mr. Komzine *(op. cit.)* its maximum output, when the bed of the Nile is completely barred and at the time of maximum floods, will rise to 11,000 cubic metres per second. 'It will be the greatest output in the world.'

In this sluice will be built 'the biggest electricity works on the African continent and one of the biggest in the world, with a power of 2,1 million kilowatts, equipped with 12 groups of 175,000 kilowatts'.

Might not the enormous mass of water in the storage lake, suspended 'above' Egypt, represent a real danger in case of war? The engineers have foreseen this threat; the level can be rapidly lowered to about 158 ft below the ridge of the artificial mountain.

It has been pointed out that the dam is in danger of being rapidly silted up by the mud it will hold back. On this point, calculations reckon it will take about five centuries to fill up the lake. As for evaporation, which is so intense in the Nubian climate, it is estimated at only 7%.

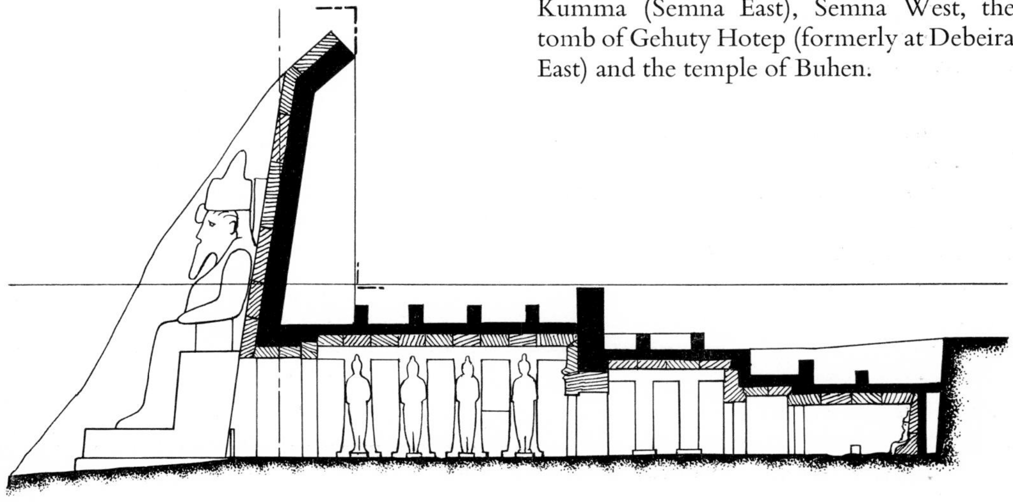

THE RECONSTRUCTION OF THE MONUMENTS AND THEIR NEW SITES

The monuments of Nubia which were dismantled will be rebuilt on four main sites. These sites will be turned into oases, so that the monuments will rapidly have the advantage of natural scenery. These 'oasis' museums will be situated:

1. *Near Aswan.* There we shall be able to see the reconstructed temple of Kalabsha. The 'kiosk' of Kertassi is also there, but as it was rebuilt too close to the preceding monument, it will undoubtedly by moved a little further away on the same site. The temple of Beit el Wali is there, too.
2. *Near the former site of Wadi es Sebui.* The temples of Wadi es Sebui and Dakka will rise on this new site.
3. Near the former site of Amada. Here we shall see the temple of Amada and the Tomb of Pennut.
4. *On the height of Abu Simbel.* The two temples of Abu Simbel, the monuments of Gebel Chams and Abu Oda will be assembled here. The monuments of Sudanese Nubia will be re-installed in a park laid out near Khartoum, around a stretch of water imitating the Nile. They are: Aksha (bas-reliefs), Kumma (Semna East), Semna West, the tomb of Gehuty Hotep (formerly at Debeira East) and the temple of Buhen.

TWO EXAMPLES OF RESCUE OPERATIONS

A) THE RELOCATION OF AMADA

The salvage of the temple of Amada would be worth a long study on its own. It was, in fact, a remarkably successful operation.

The U.A.R. dismantled the fore-part (pronaos) of the temple: the dismantled sections were transported to the future site without difficulty. But the massive part of the building still had to be transferred. This involved extracting a block some 80 by 32 ft, weighing 800 tons and 3,000 years old. Then the block had to be moved 2,800 yards and raised at its terminus from the 127 metre level to the 191 metre level, a difference of 65 metres. Instead of removal by river, it was decided (on the advice of M. Trouvelot, Inspector General of French Historical Monuments) to transfer it by land on wheels. First of all a ditch was dug around the temple. Thus it was isolated on a sort of natural hill, which became a support formed of the existing sandstone. This natural support was replaced by a chequer-work of beams of pre-stressed concrete.

Four more pre-stressed concrete beams were then arranged as follows: one lined the rear wall of the temple; two more lined its two side walls; the last one penetrated via the temple door to the rear of the sanctuary. These supporting beams were mounted on eleven jacks (each of them capable of carrying 120 tons).

These eleven jacks were mounted on eleven trolleys which moved on three parallel sets of rails. The whole thus formed a mobile group which, in the best conditions, could cover 150 ft per day and climb slopes of 5%. The eleven jacks 'wiped out' the unevennesses which remained on the terrain prepared by a limited amount of digging (only 3,000 cubic metres of rocks were removed over a distance of 2,800 yards).

The building had been consolidated in advance by injections of cement in the joints of the blocks which composed it. It was 'tied up' with chains to hold it together like a parcel.

All this care explains how the firm of Sainrapt and Brice, the engineer J. Prévost, in association with the Misr Concrete Development Company of Cairo, were able to take the temple to its new site, without one inch of its sculptures, reliefs and paintings having suffered. The operation was financed by France to the tune of 237,350 dollars.

B) THE SAVING OF ABU SIMBEL

Of all the problems posed by the salvage of the Nubian Monuments, the problem of Abu Simbel was the most difficult to solve. The salvage of the two temples of Ramesses II proved quite indispensable if it was desired that the most convincing proof of the royal power over these remote lands should remain. Together with Philae, perhaps even more, the group at Abu Simbel – need we remind the reader? – is the monumental masterpiece of Nubia. How could these two temples be saved? As you will remember each temple was a speos, in other words a building hollowed out of and installed in the sandstone cliff, preceded by high megalithic façades. The great temple in particular seemed to defy the technicians. We can understand that they looked on it as a challenge. They had to meet it.

As a result, various projects were worked out, proposed, studied. First of all French technicians (Coyne-Bellier) studied the putting into practise of a project which some called 'classical'. The site was to be preserved by the erection of a vast semi-circular rock fill dam, abutting onto the rock face at two

points upstream and downstream from the two temples. Naturally, the external level of the water, after the construction of the Sadd el Aali, would not have reached the top of this protective dam.
The disadvantages of such a project led to its being abandoned – probably rather too hastily, it seems. People objected that the site and the two buildings would look as if they were at the bottom of a basin (in spite of the dimensions of the protective dam, in spite of its gentle slopes, in spite of the sheet of water reserved at the foot of the temples so that they would reflected in it). From the archaeological point of view the dam wall would act as a screen to the rising sun. Thus the great temple would be deprived of the lighting which was so arranged by the Pharaoh's architects that the statues of the naos were illuminated twice a year.
As for the technicians, they were afraid of the risk of infiltration beneath the protective dam. True, they envisaged the installation of a pumping station to counteract it ... but its construction would have increased the global cost of the project. And it was the costly nature of the undertaking which alienated a number of experts. Many archaeologists regretted and still regret its abandonment. Indeed the French solution had a considerable advantage in its favour: it did not displace the monuments and so guaranteed the security of these works built of a material which had become fragile. It was the solution of prudence.

The Italian solution, new and exciting in its audacity and inventiveness, was an alternative to this project. The Italconsult company worked on it with the assistance of eminent men and scholars such as Professor Gustavo Colonetti. To quote an eminent specialist: 'While the experts weighed the advantages and risks of the French plan, a more audacious idea was submitted to them: that of the architect Piero Gazzola, who proposed to lift the whole mass. The tenacity and firmly rooted conviction of Gazzola, the assistance he was guaranteed by men of science and technicians of the stature of Gustavo Colonetti and Riccardo Morandi whose courage and competence were universally recognised and lastly the organisation of the works assumed by Italconsult finally won the day and in 1960 the General Conference of UNESCO decided to study the Italian plan which had won all the votes.
'The grandiose character of the undertaking was matched by technical ingenuity bordering on genius which made the Italian project the only one faithful to the original religious conception. After a very intensive comparative examination, a new international commission of experts chose the Italian project.
'From that point the essential thing was to collect the necessary funds ... an insuperable difficulty which caused the failure of the plan.'

The idea was to surround the two temples with a strong framework of concrete and at the same time to ensure the internal solidity of the monuments by various means. The buildings, transformed into independent blocks of rocks, would be set up on a substructure resting on hundreds of jacks.
These jacks would look after the raising of the two edifices to the site where they would be out of the reach of the floods. In this way each temple would be on a sort of pedestal. A landscape would be 'reconstructed' around them.
This Italian project was also very expensive. It was abandoned, even though it had passionate and enlightened partisans.
A third solution – French – was put forward. Like the Italian one, it was highly original. Caquot, an engineer, suggested setting up the temples detached from the rock inside a concrete tank built around them. An increase in the volume of water introduced into the tanks would be used to raise them. Putting it extremely simply, it was claimed

that each edifice would become a sort of float which would rise to the higher level of the new site chosen.
Here again the project was abandoned because of its cost and the practical difficulties. In the end a fourth solution won the deciding votes. Adopted in 1963, it is now being carried out. Worked out by the Swedish company Vattenbyggnadsbyrån, it was put in the hands of the *International Joint Venture,* a consortium including Hochtief of Essen, Egyptian, Swedish, Italian and French firms. In the course of a preliminary operation the rocky mass situated above the temples will be removed. They will thus be freed from their geological attachment. Then they will be cut up into sections.
These sections will be loaded onto special lorries and transported to a large zone where they will be stocked. Then they will be retransported to a site chosen on the cliff. There they will be reassembled and the temples will be rebuilt. This place is 64 metres above the present temple and 180 metres farther back.
Then the actual framework will be reconstructed. The structure of reinforced concrete which will surround and hold together all the sections will be topped with concrete vaults capable of supporting a facing of rocks. The main advantage of this project is its relatively modest price (between 32 and 36 million dollars). In addition, twice a year, the tourist will be able to see the morning sunlight penetrate into the temple as far as the gods of the sanctuary, just as before. Does this mean that we are not entitled to make reservations? Does not Abu Simbel risk losing its character? We subscribe to the view of M. Pierre Ichac who, in his book on *Le Grand Barrage d'Assouan,* wrote so justly: 'The Egyptian and Swedish project for cutting up, transporting in separate sections and rebuilding the temples on top of the plateau... has in its favour the fact that it is relatively simple, only poses elementary problems of transport and is immeasurably much cheaper than the others. On the other hand, in the eyes of archaeologists and lovers of art, it destroys for ever the quasi geological unity which made Abu Simbel a great artistic site unrivalled in the world. We may say that when the temples are relocated, the soul of Abu Simbel will have vanished.'
No doubt, but nevertheless we should be thankful for a solution which saves the temples from destruction. The undertaking is a considerable one: the total weight to be transported is about 15,000 tons (small temple of Nefertari: 3,500 tons; great temple 11,500 tons). Because of the fragility of the sandstone it is being reinforced by massive injections of synthetic resins. Lastly, it has been necessary to build a temporary dam 360 metres long, which will protect the works, for they cannot be completed in less than six years, by which time the Nile will have reached its new level of expansion.
In a few years, boats and hydroplanes will take people from Aswan to Abu Simbel in a few hours. Travellers will no longer see Nubia as it was, as we have tried to show it in this book. But the great temples will be preserved in their essentials – and in spite of everything their beauty will be saved.

Illustrations

1 *Philae.* Detail of a capital with floral decoration.

2 *Abu Simbel.* Great temple. Façade. Nefertari, 'Great Royal Wife of Ramesses II'. She is depicted standing, to the right of the entrance to the temple, beside the lower part of the king's leg.

3 *Philae.* Bas-relief on the eastern tower of the first pylon (fragment). The goddess Isis.

4 *Philae.* Interior of the temple of Isis. Columns with scenes of offerings.

5 *Ramesses II.* Turin Museum. Diorite. The king, dressed in a pleated linen robe, here wears the ceremonial crown decorated with small circles. In his right hand, the crook. His shoulders are engraved with two cartouches containing his prenomen and surname respectively. (Photograph, Rampazzi, Turin.)

6 *Dakka.* Bas-relief. The God Nile offering the plants symbolic of Upper and Lower Egypt.

7 *Kalabsha.* Bas-relief of the God Nile (fragment).

8 The valley of the Nile, upstream from Abu Simbel. Aerial view.

9 The Nile at Aswan and the island of Elephantine.

10 What the villages of Lower Nubia were like. A lighter band half way up the sandstone in the foreground marks the level reached by the Nile during the high water period. Below, the narrow green strip of crops cultivated during the brief period of low water *(coloured plate).*

11 Landscape in Lower Nubia before the construction of the new dam *(coloured plate).*

12 Village of former Lower Nubia. Walls built of mud from the Nile.

13 Rock formations upstream from Aswan.

14 House in a village of former Lower Nubia. Above the door the marks left by plates which were used for decoration and removed when the village was evacuated.

15 Panoramic view of Nubia from the Second Cataract to the First Cataract and beyond, by Horeau.

PHILAE

16 Floral capital of a column of the *mammisi,* surmounted with a cube showing the face of the goddess Hathor.

17 The colonnade of the *mammisi*. Columns with floral capitals showing the face of Hathor, beneath the representation of a temple. In the background the island of Bigah. Half way up it, the lighter band which indicates the level of high water. Photograph taken in the second fortnight of October. The left of the photograph leads to the south.

18 Monumental gateway of the temple of Isis, dominated by the traditional gorge and decorated with scenes of offerings. On either side, on the walls of the first pylon, effigies of the goddess Hathor. The effigy on the left was effaced when Egypt became Christian. The transformation of the temple into a church also explains the cross inscribed in a circle which can be seen on the right-hand upright of the door, at water level. Through the monumental door can be seen the inside courtyard, then the door of the second pylon and one of the effigies of Hathor which surround it. The photograph shows how the second part of the monument is set back in a S.W. – N.E. direction.

19 Temple of Isis. Western tower of the first pylon. Pharaoh preparing to massacre the prisoners he holds in his left hand. The conquered implore his mercy. Bas-relief chiselled out in the Christian period.

20 Eastern tower of the second pylon. Note, low down on the right, the semicircular surface of the granite block which was dressed and polished to take an inscription.

21 First pylon of the great temple of Isis. North face. Bas-relief representing one of the carriers of the sacred boat. (Part of the hull appears above, right.) Fragment.

22 Landing-stage of Nectanebo, on the southern tip of the island. In the background the island of Bigah.

23 Small temple of Hathor. In the background the east bank.

24 The island of Philae at the end of the nineteenth century, before the construction of the first Aswan dam. (Roger-Viollet.)

25 Bas-relief on the second pylon of the great temple of Isis, east face. Detail.

26 Bas-relief on one of the columns of the sanctuary.

27 Drawing of a relief decorating a chapel undoubtedly consecrated to Osiris (west side of the great temple of Isis). Description p. 62 and 67.

28 Left, supported on the magic knot, the hippopotamus goddess Ta-urt (Thoueris), with her large flanks, symbol of fecundity (she was invoked during childbirth), but also of the dense force which destroys. Right, the bird-soul. (See pl. 55.)

29 Temple of Osiris on the island of Bigah.

30 The island of Bigah, west of Philae. The temple from the Graeco-Roman period, consecrated to Osiris, and the village of Bigah (1961).

31 Portal of the temple of Osiris, on the island of Bigah. The bas-reliefs represent scenes of offerings.

32 Colonnade of the kiosk of Trajan.

33 Drawing of a bas-relief depicting 'Osiris vegetating'.

34 *Philae.* The great temple of Isis, front view, preceded by the landing-stage and pavilion of Nectanebo (left), and by the two porticoes which demarcate a dromos, to left and right. Right, the kiosk of Trajan. Between the kiosk and the great temple, the small temple of Hathor *(coloured plate).*

35 *Philae,* from the slopes of the island of Bigah. From right to left: landing-stage and pavilion of Nectanebo, west and east porticoes; kiosk of Trajan, first pylon; *mammisi,* inside court, building with a portico; second pylon; hypostyle hall of the pronaos; naos. Abutting onto the buildings on the left, additional chapel. On the first pylon, note, left, the small door communicating with the *mammisi (coloured plate).*

36 *Philae.* Portal of the naos *(coloured plate).*

37 *Philae.* Bas-relief on a column. Offering scene *(coloured plate).*

38 *Philae.* Façade of the second pylon, seen from the west. Right, the *mammisi (coloured plate).*

39 Diagrams of Philae.

PRELUDE TO KALABSHA

40 *Debod.*

41 Chapel of *Kertassi.*

42 Chapel of *Tafa.*
These three photographs were supplied by the Centre for Documentation on Ancient Egypt, Cairo.

KALABSHA

43 The temple at the period of low water. The light band on the pylon shows the level which was reached by the annual submersion after the construction of the first Aswan dam.

44 Bird's-eye view of the temple as seen from the slope which dominated it to the west.

45–46 Setting up scaffolding. The beginning of the work of 'cutting up' the temple.

47 In the inside courtyard, portal and façade of the hypostyle hall of the naos, looking towards the naos. The work preparatory to the removal of the building has begun.

48 Bas-relief. Horus-Pharaoh wearing the double crown of Upper and Lower Egypt presents a figurine of Maat, symbol of Justice and Truth, and holds the Seth-headed sceptre.

49 Bas-relief. Holding the finger to the mouth and the tress of hair symbolise childhood. The crown worn by the god-Pharaoh, on the other hand, represents the war-cry.

50 Bas-relief. Outside wall of the sanctuary.

51 The bas-relief of the 'two Mandulises'.

52 Bas-relief. Wall of the naos. Offering scene.

53 Bas-relief. The suckling of the infant Horus.

54 The temple during the months of high water. Only the cornices and the tops of the pylon and the hypostyle hall emerged. Left, in the boat, the first expedition led by the author (1960).

55 Bas-relief of the bird-soul.

56 Bas-relief. Isis. Wall of the ambulatory.

BEIT EL WALI

57 Entrance of the sanctuary. On the uprights, an inscription: 'The Sun loves him who loves The Sun'.

58 Bas-reliefs in the court: Ramesses II, on his throne, receives the submission and the

tribute of the conquered peoples of the south.

59 Bas-reliefs in the court: the peoples of the south bring their tribute to Ramesses (detail).

60 First hall of the speos. In the niche, the king between Isis and Horus. Right, on the wall, a painting: the king offers a figurine of Maat.

61 First hall of the speos. Proto-Doric column.

62 Bas-relief in the passage leading to the second hall. The personage on the left wears the headdress of the Delta, the one on the right the mitre of Upper Egypt; this is probably a depiction of the 'reunion' of the two countries.

63 *Beit el Wali*. Bas-reliefs in the court. From the coloured casts by Joseph Bonomi (British Museum). Above, the king, followed by his sons, charges and puts to flight the people of the land of Kush (south wall). Below, the gifts brought to the king in token of submission (lower register: monkeys, panthers, giraffe, oxen with deformed horns ending in hands, antelopes, etc. Upper register: shields, seats, precious woods, ivory tusks, ostrich feathers, lion, greyhounds, etc. *(coloured plate)*.

64 House in *Lower Nubia* with paintings and inscriptions on the whitewashed mud walls *(coloured plate)*.

DAKKA

65 The temple as it appeared at the period of low water.

66 The temple seen from the south-east.

67 The pylon seen from the axis of the dromos.

68 Internal façade of the pylon seen from the pronaos.

69 Portico of the pronaos.

70 View looking towards the naos, with the stone tabernacle appearing in the centre.

71 Bas-relief on the façade of the pronaos, lower register to the west. The gifts of the Nile.

72 Bas-reliefs on the façade of the pronaos. East side. Scenes of offerings.

73 Bas-reliefs on the façade of the pronaos. West side. Scenes of offerings.

74 Bas-relief: Anukis, goddess of the First Cataract.

A CHANGE OF TACK
GERF HUSSEIN, DENDUR

75 *Gerf Hussein*. The king as Osiris. Statue in the pronaos.

76 *Gerf Hussein*. Temple of Ptah. Court and portico.

77 Dendur. Temple of Pedesi and Pihor. (These last three photographs were supplied by the Centre for Documentation on Ancient Egypt, Cairo.)

THE LIONS AND THE SAND: WADI ES SEBUI

78 Sphinx, with crowned Horus-falcon head, protecting the Pharaoh.

79 The temple as it appeared at the period of low water.

80 The temple at the period of high water.

81 Pylon of the temple. In the background, still erect statue of Ramesses II, accompanied by the effigy of a princess (more accurately one of his daughters, whom he was to marry). In the foreground, fallen colossus of Ramesses. On the left, it rests on the rod of authority which terminates at face height in a falcon head.

82 Close-up of the head of the same colossus. Above, right, upper part of the broken *shent*.

83 Sphinx lining the dromos.

84 Head of sphinx.

85 Inside court. Portal of the pronaos transformed in the Christian period by filling in and the addition of a double opening.

86 Portico, south side of the court. Pillars showing Ramesses as Osiris.

87 Bas-relief in the speos. The sovereign offers incense to four seated deities (from left to right: Nekhbet, Tefnut, the king himself, Onuris).

88 Bas-relief. 'The offering of white bread.'

89 Painted relief in the pronaos: the goddesses Tefnut and Nekhbet.

90–91 Sphinx in the dromos.

92 Portico, south side of the court. Osirian pillar of Ramesses II.

93 *Wadi es Sebui.* The sphinxes of the dromos in the high water season *(coloured plate).*

94 *Wadi es Sebui.* Sphinx of the dromos *(coloured plate).*

RAMESSES AND THE APOSTLE

95 *Wadi es Sebui.* Niche in the *cella.* Centre, on the back wall, a painting from the Christian period: St Peter, apostle. On either side, the Pharaoh making an offering. Above the niche, the solar boat: Amun, on his throne, listens to the words of Tuth. Left, the Pharaoh kneels before the god. Right, three baboons greet the Sun.

96 *Wadi es Sebui.* Pillar bearing pharaonic hieroglyphs and a Christian image (St Michael).

THE CEMETERY NEAR ANIBA

97 What used to be the village of *Derr* in Nubia. In the background, the mosque.

98 The citadel of *Kasr Ibrim.*

99 The temple of *Amada.*

100 Temple of *Amada.* Bas-relief. (The last two photographs were supplied by the Centre for Documentation on Ancient Egypt, Cairo.)

101 Temple of *Semna.* (Photo supplied by the Oriental Institute, University of Chicago).

BUHEN, THE FORTRESSES, THE LAND OF KUSH

102 *Buhen.* Foundations of the 18th-dynasty temple. Note that the temple (in the centre), erected in the time of Queen Hatshepsut, was surrounded by a colonnade. This simple, beautiful lay-out was altered in the reign of Tuthmosis III: the temple was enclosed with walls and it was preceded by a court surrounded by pillars. (Photograph supplied by the Oriental Institute, University of Chicago.)

103 *Buhen.* Reconstruction of the fortress (after *The Illustrated London News).*

RAMESSES II

104 Head of Ramesses II, fragment of a vanished colossus. Ramesseum (funerary temple of Ramesses II, Thebes).

105 Ramesseum, Thebes. Osirian colonnade. At the foot of the second statue, the head of Ramesses II, in profile, which we have seen front view in plate 104.

106 Ramesses II. Diorite. Turin Museum. (Provenance: Karnak. Photograph: Rampazzi, Turin.)

107 Ramesseum (Thebes). Large bas-relief on the wall preceding the hypostyle hall. Bottom register: the king's eleven sons. Centre register: left, the king is led to the temple by two deities; in the centre the god Tuth; right, the king kneels before the three

main deities of Thebes. Upper register: left, the king sacrifices to the god Ptah; right, the king makes an offering of incense to the god Min.

108 The god Tuth, in the role of man-cum-ibis. (Detail of plate 107.)

109 Ramesseum (Thebes). Inside face of the second pylon. Ramesses, standing in his chariot, bends his bow and charges the Hittites outside Kadesh.

110 Ramesseum (Thebes). Continuation of the above: battle of Kadesh; rout and massacre of the Hittites. On the lower register, arrival of the war chariots.

111 Columns of the Ramesseum (Thebes).

112 *Thebes* (Valley of the Queens). Tomb of Nefertari, the Great Wife of Ramesses II. Mural painting. The queen is introduced to the world of the Gods by Re-Harakhty *(coloured plate)*.

113 *Thebes* (Valley of the Queens). Tomb of Nefertari. Mural painting. Nefertari, Great Wife of Ramesses II performs the gesture of adoration. Right, the Heavenly Cows *(coloured plate)*.

ABU SIMBEL

114 Head of one of the four colossi of the façade (south colossus).

115 The site of Abu Simbel (aerial view) before the construction of the new dam. Left, the great temple. Centre, the stream of sand which covered part of the colossi for so long. Right, the temple of Nefertari. Note, immediately to the left of the great temple, the small door opening into the speos (chapel in the rock), and further on the surfaces on the rock reserved for inscriptions. Alongside the bank, a boat and floating laboratory. In the future the two reconstructed temples will stand on the summit of the cliff. (This photograph was taken in 1960.)

116 Façade of the great temple. Overall view.

117 Façade of the great temple. Details. Above, left: Re-Harakhti. Right: Ramesses II. Below: Queen Nefertari.

118 Façade of the great temple. In the foreground, one of the statues which decorate the edge of the terrace (Ramesses encased as Osiris).

119 Façade of the great temple. Between the legs of the colossus, the young prince Amen her Khepchef.

120 Plan of the site of Abu Simbel. Above, left: plan of the great temple in the rock. Below, right, plan of the small temple in the rock of Nefertari (after the drawing by the Centre for Documentation on Ancient Egypt, Cairo).

121 One of the feet of the south colossus of Ramesses II.

122 Façade of the great temple. Face of Queen Nefertari.

123 Façade of the great temple. Base of the first north colossus. Bas-relief of prisoners and conquered peoples of Asia and the northern regions. One knee on the ground, the captives are attached by the floral loop which symbolises Egypt. Parallel to them, but on the south side, another frieze depicts the prisoners from countries of the south.

124–125 Frieze of prisoners from Asia and the countries of the north. Details. Semitic and Hittite captives.

126 Façade of the great temple. Base of the first north colossus, to the right of the portal. The two geniuses of the Nile bind the lily and the papyrus together to symbolise the union of Upper and Lower Egypt.

127 Façade of the great temple. Horus-falcon. One of the two falcons which stand at the corners of the base of the colossi, on

either side of the passage giving access to the temple.

128 Inside court of the great temple. Osirian pillars. View looking towards the sanctuary.

129 *Abu Simbel.* Queen Mut Tyi (on the right flank of the first south colossus) *(coloured plate).*

130 *Abu Simbel.* Inside court of the great temple. South wall. Bas-relief. Ramesses II in his war chariot, launching the assault on an Asian fortress. Note the traces of painting *(coloured plate).*

131 Shepherd fleeing with his flock, beseeching Ramesses II for mercy with his hand (the shoes of the horses can be seen above, right). Detail of the preceding plate).

132–133 Path of the rising sun in the great temple.

134 The rising sun illuminates the deities in the naos.

135 Offering to Min, the generative god. On the altar, two cos lettuces. This species was supposed to have aphrodisiac powers.

136 Effigy of one of the sons of Ramesses II, between his father's feet.

137 Inside court of the great temple. Osirian pillar (detail).

138 Inside court of the great temple. Offering scene.

139 Inside court of the great temple. One of the daughters of Ramesses II, the princess Bint-Anath, playing the sistrum, instrument dear to the goddess Hathor. Nine princes are depicted in the same attitude, at the entrance to the temple, east wall, north side.

140 Inside court of the great temple. Fragment of the foundation on which is depicted a procession of eight royal sons holding a flabellum in the left hand and performing the gesture of adoration with the right hand.

141 Inside court of the great temple. South wall, central bas-relief. Ramesses fighting on foot. The king seizes a Libyan chief in his left hand and brandishes his lance in his right hand. He crushes a conquered enemy beneath his feet.

142 Detail of the preceding illustration.

143 Hieroglyphs at the entrance to the inside court.

144 *Abu Simbel.* Small temple of Nefertari. Bas-relief: Anukis, goddess of the First Cataract *(coloured plate).*

145 *Abu Simbel.* Small temple of Nefertari. Bas-relief known as the 'coronation' of Nefertari. Between the goddesses Isis and Hathor, the Queen, wearing a diadem of tall plumes, the sign of life in her right hand, becomes a goddes in her turn *(coloured plate).*

146 *Small temple or temple of the Queen.* Inside court. Pillar as effigy of the goddess Hathor. The face of the goddess is surmounted with the image of a temple, at the entrance to which rears a *uraeus.*

147 *Small temple or temple of the Queen.* Façade.

148 *Small temple or temple of the Queen.* Detail of the façade, north part: Nefertari between two effigies of Ramesses II.

149 *Small temple.* Detail of the façade. A young prince next to his father.

150 *Small temple.* Detail of the façade. Queen Nefertari.

151 *Small temple.* Scene of adoration. Nefertari holds out the sistrum to the image of the goddess Hathor.

152 *Small temple.* Ramesses receives the 'protection' of the gods Horus of Aniba and Seth.

153 *Small temple.* Nefertari making an offering of the sistrum and papyrus to Anukis.

154 *Small temple.* Detail of plate 129.

Printed in Switzerland

Contents

DATE DUE
OCT 18 1971
DEC 6 - 1971
C.T. NOV 30 1981